The Mamma Nero Diaries

A Mother's Legacy

A.D. Hyde

ISBN: 9798510506259

British Cataloguing Publication Data: A catalogue record of this book is available from The British Library.

Also available on Kindle.

Contents

A Poem for Our Mum – Margherita Hyde   7

A Poem for Chris   9

Introduction   11

Chapter 1: The Scars That Define Us   19

Chapter 2: An Italian in Manchester   29

Chapter 3: Finding Pride in the Seemingly Mundane   35

Chapter 4: Auntie Pina   40

Chapter 5: Superstitions and the Greasy Witch   51

Chapter 6: Don't Come Running to Me...   57

Chapter 7: If the Rats Don't Get You...   68

Chapter 8: The Loan Shark   81

Chapter 9: Slap Me, I'm a Fat Italian Asthmatic...   88

Chapter 10: The Magic of Food   93

Chapter 11: The Ouija Board   101

Chapter 12: The Ice Cream Wars and Free Ice Cream   113

Chapter 13: What, No Garlic?   119

Chapter 14: An Englishman's Home is His Castle...   125

Chapter 15: From Hairy Jumpers to Racing Pigeon Pie   135

Chapter 16: Dementia, Noisy Postmen and Care Homes   150

Chapter 17: The Legacy   161

Words of Wisdom   165

Acknowledgements   168

More From The Author   169

Coming Soon   170

About the Author   171

This book is dedicated to my mother,
and to my brother Chris.

A Poem for Our Mum – Margherita Hyde

We didn't know the story before us
We didn't know of the pain and the loss
Why would we? She was just our mum
We didn't see her in front, holding back the storm
We didn't see that while we were eating... she was not
Why would we? She was just our mum
We didn't see the inner strength
or the sacrifices she made
We didn't see the fear for our safety
or the hope for our future
Why would we? She was just our mum
Now as parents we see
Now as parents we truly know
She was strong, courageous, selfless and proud...
but still... she was just our mum

A.D. Hyde, 2021

A Poem for Chris

I'll go first and make sure it's safe, he said...
You come when you're ready
But don't rush, because you've got things to do
They have free ale on tap
And an *all you can eat buffet*
You come when you're ready
But don't rush, because you have things to do
There will be lots of friends there
And lots of stories to tell
You come when you're ready
But don't rush, because you've got things to do
...he said he'd go first and make sure it was safe

A.D. Hyde, 2019

Introduction

My earliest memory is of my first day at school; I was about four years old and I remember holding my mother's hand as she walked me into the school playground. It's such a vivid memory that it could have happened yesterday.

The playground was bathed in sunshine and packed with kids of all ages. Some were playing games, some were huddled in groups, some were chasing each other around and some were just... well... in their own little worlds, oblivious to the mayhem that surrounded them. There were girls skipping, boys playing football and just about every other activity you can think of. And in the middle, towering over all of them like a lighthouse in a stormy sea, was a giant of a man. He had a bushy well-kept beard, a stout belly and a shiny metal whistle in his mouth. His face was red with the effort of shouting and blowing his whistle. The shrill scream from the whistle was directed at a scruffy boy who was trying to scare a bunch of girls by thrusting a rather large frog into their faces. "Jenkins! Stop that! Jenkins! Are you listening to me? If I've told you once, I've told you a thousand times... girls do not like kissing frogs! *Now put it down...* **now**!"

He turned his attention to an older girl who had just come through the school gates. "Tracey! Make up is not part of the school uniform, is it?... No... and that skirt is far too short... Go and stand outside the headmaster's office." A tough-looking boy was pulling faces behind the man's back and his friends were all laughing and goading him on, until the man said: "Don't think I can't see you, Jones... Detention!" The boy was stunned and turned to his mates with his arms stretched out, as if to say, 'How on earth did he see me? He really does have eyes in the back of his head!'

"Right... Williamson! That's the last time I'm going to tell you to get off the wall. Don't come running to me if you break both your legs." It was like I was watching a film, or, to be more precise, it was like I was in the film, but no one could see me. Until, that is, the giant turned and looked directly at me. "Hello, you're new. Is this your first day?" I just stood there with my mouth open. Actually... that's a little misleading, because I had asthma, so I always had my mouth open. Let's just say, I was stunned and motionless. I was like this for many reasons: firstly, because I had no idea why I was there. I wouldn't have put it past my mum to have said nothing at all. Secondly, I didn't know whether I was 'new' or not... and thirdly, he scared the crap out of me!

That giant's name was Mr Wadsworth. He was well over six feet tall and built like a rugby player. Initially he came across as a very intimidating person indeed, but later I would learn that he was a great teacher who commanded respect. He would turn out to be the most influential teacher from my early years, and the sad thing is that he would never know it.

There was an incident a few years after our first encounter in the playground. I was in his class and he called me over to his desk and told me to take off my shoes. I thought I had done something wrong and he was going to punish me. We were very poor, and my mum could barely afford to feed and clothe my siblings and me. I guess there would be times that I probably looked scruffy and bedraggled... *not that I knew or cared.* On this particular day, I was perhaps a bit more bedraggled than usual. Anyway, I took off my shoes and handed them to him, as requested. He stared at my feet and then back at me. It was then that I realised I had a hole in my sock... and my big toe was poking out. I was a bit embarrassed and put my other foot over it. He looked at the shoes I had given him, and his face darkened... Looking back now, I can see that what I thought I saw in his face as anger towards me was in fact anger at my situation. He took my left shoe, put his hand inside and poked his finger through the rather large hole in the sole. He went on to do the same with my right shoe. Then he sighed and his face softened to reveal a warm smile. "This won't do, will it?" he said. He pulled a piece of thick card from his desk, cut out a shoe-shaped piece and placed it into the shoe he was holding. Then he did the same for my other shoe, before helping me put my shoes back on. He straightened my tie and shirt collar... ruffled my hair... smiled again and said: "Go on, back to your desk."

Mr Wadsworth taught me a lot during those early years. He taught me to look beneath the surface. He taught me that beneath the most intimidating and off-putting exterior often lies the warmest and most beautiful soul. If I look at the majority of my closest friends today, they are tall and imposing figures... and, in some cases, you might say intimidating... but beneath the surface they are warm and true. I am always drawn to the beauty inside, irrespective of what the exterior looks like.

Back to the schoolyard. I was awakened from my stunned state by my mother, who said: "I am Margherita Hyde, and this is Anthony. It's his first day; where do I take him?" It's probably worth mentioning at this point that my mother spoke English with a very thick Italian accent, which meant that no one outside her close circle of family and friends had a clue what she was saying. For example, if she was going to ask you whether you wanted any butter on your toast, she would say, "Wonna some butt?" She would also slip the odd Italian word into a sentence, just to make sure she really confused people. "Vieni qui... I fixa," which, roughly translated, meant "Come here and I'll fix it."

I can imagine that Mum's simple question would have sounded like a foreign language to the uninitiated. And, indeed, I suspect now that Mr Wadsworth had no idea what she had just said. Credit to him though, because he thought for a while, then said: "Why don't you take your son to Mrs Brown's class?" and pointed to a door at the end of the playground. When in doubt, pass the problem on.

The next thing I remember is standing in front of that big brown imposing wooden door (I guess any door is imposing to a four-year-old). My mother pushed open the door and led me into a large classroom full of screaming children and concerned parents. This should have been a frightening moment in my life, because I had never experienced anything like this before. Up until this point, I had been cocooned in our small terraced house. The only bit of the outside world I had seen was a small section of the cobbled street outside our front door. I had never seen this many people in one place before, but I wasn't scared. In fact,

I distinctly remember feeling calm
all. Again, looking back now, it w
knew why they were there. Their
tell them that this was their firs
momentous day – the day they
enlightenment and education. The
that they would be left on their own with a group o
all day! That's why they were crying. Whereas I had no idea
what was going to happen and certainly no idea that my
mum was going to leave me there all day, so I was chilled.

My attention was suddenly diverted by a deafening bell.
It was probably the loudest and most painful sound I had
ever heard. I put my hands to my ears to protect them and of
course closed my eyes tightly... I've never understood why
closing your eyes could possibly help protect against a loud
sound, but closed they stayed, until the bell stopped. When I
opened my eyes, I noticed that most of the parents had left.
The only parents remaining were the ones with hysterical
kids clinging to their legs. I turned to my mother to ask her
what was going on... only to realise that she had buggered
off! Now, she may have said goodbye, but it certainly isn't
part of my vivid recollection – but there was a lot going on
that day. The other weird thing about this 'vivid' memory is
that I have no recollection of looking up at Mum. The
memory just has her from the waist down, like the teacher in
the Charlie Brown cartoons.

Mum was very protective and caring, but she was also
strong and self-reliant, so she couldn't empathise with
people who were helpless (an attribute which I have also
inherited). So, I can imagine her leaving me there without

saying anyth...
wasn't a b...
irritated
them

ing, because as far as she was concerned it ~~ig deal. I also suspect that she would have been . by all the crying kids and the parents mollycoddling

As the last of the parents managed to tear themselves way, I remembered not understanding why the kids were still crying. I can hear you say, "What? Your mother has just left you in a strange place with lots of crying kids and you're not that bothered? I don't believe it!" My response is... *you didn't know my mum.* She was convinced that in order to protect her children she had to stop them doing anything that was even remotely dangerous. My childhood memories are swamped with phrases like "Don't do that!" ... "Come away from that!" ... "Don't eat that!" ... "Put that down!" ... "Stop doing that, you'll go blind!" So, anytime I was away from my mum's controlling influence I found it to be quite liberating, and this was no exception.

I want to make something crystal clear to you before you go away thinking that my mother was a cold, uncaring human being, because she wasn't. She was loving, loyal and selfless. Family was everything to her and she would protect the ones she loved at the expense of her own health and happiness. But in order to survive all the hardships in her life, she had to get tough.

So, if you asked me to describe my childhood, I would initially choose words like hardship, poor, excluded, different and lonely. But, with the benefit of age and the knowledge of my mother's story, I would still use words like hardship and poor, but I would add words like privileged, inspiring and unique. I am the product of my mother and my social upbringing. I have strong principles of loyalty and honesty. Family is the most important thing in my life, and I would do anything to protect the ones I love. I appreciate everything I have, because I know what it's like to have nothing. I am what I am because of my mother and she was, well... above all, she was a strong *Italian mamma*. She was proud, selfless, independent, resourceful, stubborn, and above all, a little bit of a nutter.

What did she teach me and my siblings? Well...

- She taught us that if a pigeon with a ring around its ankle lands in your back yard it means God wants you to make a pie tonight.
- She taught us that if people come to visit you should feed them... even if it means that you go hungry the day after... and when they leave, you give them any remaining food, along with the plates it was on.
- She taught us that the best way to end an argument was to smash all the plates and cups that were left over from the last lot of people who came to visit.
- She taught us to buy cheap crockery.
- She taught us it was a crime to run out of tomato puree.
- She taught us how to make great chips!
- She taught us that the best way to keep vampires away was to place an upturned broom against your bedroom door.
- She taught us that if you come home one day and find your father in bed with a strange naked woman,

she's obviously a witch and you should push her out of the first storey bedroom window and watch her crawl away in agony. (Keep reading, full story to come!)

- She taught us that, no matter how bad things get, you never give up on yourself... If life knocks you down, admit defeat. Have a cry, lick your wounds... then get up and get on with it.
- She taught us to have faith... faith that things will get better.
- She taught us that while an Englishman's home is his castle, an Italian's castle is his family.

Words of Wisdom: Look beneath the surface, because under the most intimidating exterior can often be found the warmest and most amazing soul.

Chapter 1
The Scars That Define Us

Mum with her younger brother Atillio

Even though Mum ended her days as a small and frail old lady, I will always remember her as a formidable *Italian mamma*. Etched on the back of my mind is an image of a short stocky middle-aged Italian woman with rugged features. She has strong cheek bones... the sort of cheekbones that celebrities would pay a lot of money for. Her hair is like wire-wool, mainly due to years and years of applying ultra-strong hair spray. This hair offered the impact protection of a motorbike helmet and the flammability of a giant match. Her hands are an artist's dream; they look as though Michelangelo himself carved them from granite. I remember getting slapped by those hands... my ears are still ringing now. Yet when she smiles, her face lights up and all those rugged features melt away to reveal her inner warmth and beauty. The rigours of life had shaped her inside and out, but they couldn't diminish her true self.

She was born on the twenty first of October 1932, in a small village called Liberi, which is situated in the hills about forty kilometres inland from Naples. I was going to say her early years were hard, but let's face it... just about all her years were hard. So let's just say that her early years were some of her hardest. She grew up through a fascist government, unbearable poverty and a world war. But these hardships paled into insignificance when compared with the family loss she had to endure. At the age of fourteen she had to cope with the unthinkable... the loss of her mother. She didn't talk about it much; the only thing she said was that Nonna was perfectly healthy one minute and the next minute she had some sort of a fit and died instantly. No child should lose a parent, but there seems to be something more painful about a young girl losing her mother.

I'm afraid her heartache didn't end there. It seems that Nonno had his own issues even before Nonna died, which meant he found it difficult to cope afterwards. The next bit is full of conjecture, but the only thing we do know was that Mum's younger sister was taken from the family and placed in the local convent. We don't know whether this was our Nonno's decision or an authority's decision. It may have been the case that Nonno could not work anymore, they were relying on money coming in from the brothers and it was just not enough to feed everyone. It may have been the most logical decision to give my auntie a better life. She would be clothed and fed and looked after for the rest of her life. I cannot judge, because I have no real knowledge of the circumstances that led to the decision. All I can say is that, as a parent, I cannot imagine a circumstance where I would be willing to give up my child... and I cannot think of a circumstance where my heart would not break at the thought of being given away as a child.

Now think of my mum... a fourteen-year-old girl who has just lost her mother. Her father has succumbed to his own issues and his own grief and is no longer capable of heading the family the way he would want to. Then, just as she believes her heart can take no more, she has to witness her sister being taken away screaming and crying.

Now think of a seven-year-old girl who has just lost her mother. Her father is unable to comfort her... she can't possibly understand what is going on... and then, when she is at her most heartbroken and confused, the nuns come to take her away from her family – and her father, brothers and sister do nothing to stop them.

Mum didn't mention her sister much. We can't even be sure of her name, but from broken memories and scribbled notes on old bits of paper, we think she was called Teresa. We first learned about her when we were rummaging in Mum's old photos and found a picture of a beautiful young girl laid out on an altar stone. She was dressed in a white gown and had a garland of flowers around her head and flowers surrounding her body.... she looked so beautiful. When we asked Mum who she was, she started to cry and said that it was her sister. She said her father had her put into a nunnery because he couldn't look after her and the last time she spoke to her was when she went to visit her in the nunnery. Mum said that Teresa kept crying and pleading to be taken home, but they wouldn't allow Mum to take her home because she was too young. Mum said that soon after this visit her sister died *"of a broken heart"*. She then put the photograph away and said nothing more about her.

Auntie Teresa

I don't think Mum ever came to terms with her sister's death. Whether she blamed herself or just couldn't bear the loss, I don't know. I only know about loss... I wish I didn't, but I do. Losing someone who has had a full life or has suffered for a long time can be very confusing: you are heartbroken at losing them, but you are also comforted by the fact that they either had a wonderful life or that their suffering is over. However, when you lose someone quickly and way before their time, it can be an overwhelming experience. It's like you're standing in front of a door and you know that behind the door is a whole room full of pain and emotion. If you open that door when you're not ready, you will be overwhelmed by grief and the unbelievable fact that you will never see that person again. The thought of this can cause people to lock the door and protect themselves from the pain. I think Mum did this and, as a result, never really talked about her sister. She never told us what she was like, whether she was kind or mischievous or what she wanted to be when she grew up. In protecting herself, she also robbed herself of the happy memories, and she robbed her family of the chance to know this beautiful little girl.

Subconsciously, I think I learned from this. When we lost our brother Chris, the pain was so overwhelming I thought my body was shutting down; I couldn't breathe. It was then that I imagined the room... I put all the pain in the room and closed the door. I would walk past it, knowing that there was so much pain behind it. After a while I remembered that all his memories were in there too, and if I locked away the pain, I would also be locking away his memories. So, the next time I walked past the door, I opened it just a little bit and the pain was deep but bearable, because I also had a glimpse of him cooking naked... yes... he loved to cook in his boxer shorts, and I would always say: "Would you pleeeaase put some clothes on!"

Every day I would open the door wider and wider until eventually, I could take the door away. The pain will always be there, but the longer time goes on, the more it is outweighed by the happy memories. I never want to avoid a conversation about my brother; I never want people to regret mentioning his name. Every birthday and Christmas we raise a glass to Mum and Chris. I want to tell stories about them to my grandchildren, because they deserve to be remembered. I may be a logical thinker and a scientist at heart, but that doesn't stop me hoping that Mum has been reunited with her mother and her sister and that she will introduce them to her son Chris.

Mum's eldest brothers Armando and Michael

Mum sometimes talked about her life in Italy and how hard it was. She often talked about the German occupation during World War II. She would tell us about the day she was walking back home across a wheat field and how she was concentrating on looking for snakes, because they would hide in the long grass. She said she heard a 'pop' noise. I said snakes didn't go pop and she looked at me as if I was an idiot and said: "It wasn't from a snake!" She went on to say that, as she looked around the area the sound came from, she felt a bullet whistle past her ear. She panicked and jumped for cover in the long wheat. Everything went quiet and all she could hear was her heart beating and the gentle sound of the breeze blowing through the wheat... actually, she didn't say the bit about the breeze, but I thought it would create a bit of an atmosphere. Then she heard another shot, followed by a soft thud as a bullet hit the ground nearby. She said she was terrified, and she stayed as still as she could for such a long time. When she heard a group of farm labourers walking close by, she jumped up and ran as fast as she could all the way home. She went on to tell us that the Germans would often use local villagers for target practice. How evil must a person have been to indiscriminately try and kill a ten-year-old girl? Luckily, on that day, their aim was poor.

She remembered lots of fighting around that time between the Germans and the Italian resistance. She said a lot of the men from her village had to live in the mountains and the women would bring them food when they could, but of course food was scarce, and they barely had enough to feed the children. She had no love for the fascist government and even less for the German soldiers.

If my dates are correct, some of her stories would be around the time of the 'Four Days of Naples', which was in 1943 when the Italian resistance in Naples rose up against the Germans. It was after King Victor Emmanuel III deposed

Mussolini and attempted to surrender the whole of Italy to the Allied Command, but only ended up taking the south with him. Hitler wanted to keep the north and ordered five new troop divisions to bolster his existing occupying army. As the Germans relinquished the south, they did two things. The first was to free Mussolini, because Hitler wanted him to keep the local population in line, and the second was to disband all the Italian army divisions under their control. They also had a plan to destroy Naples, take the men and send them to work as slave labour in the north. The local resistance had other plans, and when the disbanded Italian army abandoned Naples, they stood fast to protect their families, their homes and their city. They were outnumbered and outgunned, but they managed to hold the Germans off until the Allied Forces arrived to relieve them. These brave resistance fighters were awarded with the Gold Medal of Military Valour for their efforts.

Mum made it through the war, but the poverty continued. Jobs were hard to find in the mountain village where she grew up, so she and her brothers Michael and Armando had to go further and further away from home to find work. She worked in Naples for a while, and it was during this time that she married and had my eldest brother Mike, named after Mum's eldest brother Michael. Again, she never talked about this period. We only know she was married in Italy because we found an annulment certificate in her papers. We have no idea when she was married, or to whom. All we do know is that the marriage was annulled before she came to England. No reason was given on the annulment certificate. This is another story I would love to know more about... but, unfortunately, there is no one to tell it.

Mum, holding my older brother Mike, with Armando and Nonno

As time went on the situation in the south worsened, to the extent that Mum, Michael and Armando had to take jobs even further from home. This in turn meant that she had to stay away from her son, Mike, for extended periods. What else could she do? If she'd stayed home, she would have found it very difficult to earn enough money to feed and clothe Mike. So she had no other option but to leave Mike with her father and her younger brother Attilio and follow the work. This led her north through Italy, into France, then Geneva and finally she made her way to Manchester, England... to begin the next chapter of her life.

Words of Wisdom: One of my favourite lyrics is from a Bob Marley song: "You never know how strong you are until being strong is the only choice you have."

Chapter 2

An Italian in Manchester

Mum arrived in England on the second of September 1959. She was accompanied by her younger brother Armando and, together, they were embarking on a new beginning... a new life. This wasn't just another place to find work; this was going to be a place to put down roots. They were fortunate that their eldest brother Michael had already made the journey and was living and working in Manchester. He had also managed to find them both jobs in the local cotton mill and until they could find a place of their own, they were to stay with him. It must have been great for Mum to have her brothers with her.

Michael, Armando and Mum were at the tail end of a post-war wave of Italian emigration to the UK. There was still huge demand in the textile industry for workers, because they could not meet worldwide demand for their products and were running the mills twenty-four hours a day. It was hard work in the mills, but that was a price they were more than willing to pay, because the alternative was to return to the poverty they were escaping back in Italy.

The Italian migrants came with the dream of making a new and better life for themselves... but unfortunately, it wasn't all plain sailing. Yes, the jobs and the money were there, but the local residents still harboured resentment towards them for the role they played in World War II.

Consequently, those first-generation immigrants found it hard to integrate into the local community, which is why they created their own communities... their own 'Little Italies'. These were areas where they could feel at home, where they could meet friends and have a pizza and a decent cup of coffee... a place where they could feel safe. *Little Italy* in Manchester must have been a welcome haven for Mum and her brothers. After all, they were in a strange country, with strange food and strange customs. The weather was cold and wet, and of course they didn't speak the language very well. Mum had the added pressure that she was on a six-month visa, and she was concerned that she would be kicked out when those six months were up. If it was just her, that wouldn't have been so bad – but she wanted to make this move permanent so she could send for her son.

Life has a habit of opening a door just when and where you need it. The door that opened for Mum was the one that let my dad through. He was seventeen years old and worked in the same cotton mill. He must have been knocked off his feet by this twenty-seven-year-old Mediterranean woman. Things moved swiftly and, after a whirlwind romance, they were married. Oh... and I missed out the bit where they were married just before Mum's visa expired. I know what you're thinking... but we will never know.

Within days of getting married, Mum sent word back to Italy: "Bring Michael." At last she would be reunited with her son. It was my Nonno who brought three-year-old Michael over from Italy. Finally, my mum had her son, she was married, and she had a home... Life was great.

Mum

Her family would soon expand with the addition of my brother Chris, then me, then my sister Diane. For a time, she must have thought she was living a dream when she compared it to the life she had in Italy. But yes, you guessed it... her dream turned into a nightmare when the marriage broke down and my parents divorced when I was about two years old.

I have no memories of my dad when I was growing up. He never visited us, and we never visited him... not that we knew where he lived. It wasn't until I was nineteen that I eventually met him. My brother Chris arranged a meeting for us all with him in a pub near where he lived. I must admit, I went more out of curiosity than a desire to get to know my father. The curiosity was more specifically a question... and the question was: "Why did you never make contact?" All the time I was growing up, not once did he come and see us – and he only lived ten or fifteen miles away. Why am I telling you this? Because events like this have shaped my life and shaped the person I am. I don't know the reason for their divorce. I don't know what my mother was like to live with as a wife, and I don't know what my father was like to live with as a husband. I know that few people are lucky enough to meet someone they can truly spend the rest of their life with. I know that people change, and that they can sometimes wake up one morning and decide the person they married is no longer the person they want to spend the rest of their life with. I can understand and sympathise with all that... but where I lose sympathy is when a parent severs all ties with their children after a divorce.

I didn't ask my father why and he didn't tell me why. He just acted as though nothing had happened. To be honest, there wouldn't have been an excuse good enough for me. If it were me, I would have found a way to see my children and let them know that I loved them and that I would always be there for them. I think he thought he could just carry on regardless. I think he thought the door was open for him to be a part of my life, to be my father again. But what actually happened was... that meeting closed a long-open door in my life. He was not my father... he was just a man... and a man I had nothing in common with.

Writing this book has revealed to me how life events you experience as a child can affect the adult in one of two ways: you find yourself scared by them in a negative way or moulded in a positive way. For example, you can either find yourself repeating the mistakes of your parents, or you can learn from them and make a new path. I subconsciously and consciously learned from them. I learned that family was everything... it was worth sacrificing your life for. From a very early age, I vowed that I would find the woman of my dreams and I would love her with every ounce of my being. I also vowed that if I was ever lucky enough to have children, they would know that no matter what the future brings, their father would always be there for them.

So... back to the timeline... and Margherita Hyde finds herself single with four children to raise. She can't afford the rent on the house where she lives, so she moves in with her brother Armando until she can find somewhere that she can afford. It wasn't long before the council gave her a 'two up, two down' terraced house in Ashton-under-Lyne, where the majority of my childhood memories would be made.

Words of Wisdom: All it takes to earn the eternal love of a dog is a biscuit and a hug... but to earn the love of a child, you need a lifetime of sacrifice.

Chapter 3

Finding Pride in the Seemingly Mundane

I described Mum's hands as being carved from stone, which was slightly inaccurate, because they were more like stone covered with sandpaper. Those hands are prominent in another of my vivid childhood memories. For some reason, one day I couldn't go into school and she couldn't take time off work, so she had to take me with her. I remember her getting me ready and saying that today was going to be a special day for me and that I had to be very good. She packed my paper and pencils in a bag and said I could sit and draw while she worked. She made some sandwiches for us both and we went off to catch the bus. I felt as though everyone was looking at me, as though they all knew that I was going to work with my mum. The bus was crowded and a bit smelly, so I was glad when it stopped and Mum took my hand to lead me off. The bus had stopped right outside these huge black iron gates. The gates were open wide, and hundreds of people were flowing through to the red brick cotton mill beyond. And here is the really spooky bit... I have another memory of those same gates, but thirty years later.

I had started work for a company called Courtaulds in Coventry. Amongst other things, they owned many of the old cotton mills around the country. As part of my induction process I was sent to one of those mills to see how they manufactured nylon. Even after I was given the address, I didn't think anything of it, other than it was back in Manchester and I could visit Mum while I was there. But as I drove up to the address I was given, I had to stop the car. I had stopped just in front of a pair of huge black iron gates... it was the same factory that Mum had worked at. It still sends shivers down my spine now.

Back to the first time I saw those gates. We joined a queue of people walking through the entrance to the mill. As they went through the double doors they calmly merged into single file. Then, one by one, they took it in turns to go through a turnstile. Just before they went through, they each picked a card from a pouch on the wall and put it into what looked like an old clock. There was a stamp and a ping, and the card was removed. Once they were through the turnstile, they put the card in another pocket on the wall. Then it was our turn, and Mum did the same as all the others. I attracted quite a few looks as I went through. I guess it wasn't normal to bring your children to work in those days.

After getting through the turnstile we followed a stream of women who were making their way into a room on the left. As we got closer, the noise from the room got louder and louder until we entered and the noise was almost painful. The room was huge... probably the size of two or three tennis courts. And there were rows and rows of machines, which were used to load nylon onto little bobbins. Mum led me to her work station, where she was taking over from a woman who had just worked the night shift. The woman smiled at me, said something to Mum about a loose pulley wheel and left. Mum sat me close to the window with my pen and paper. Then, before she could take her coat off, a man came over with a stern look on his face. He and Mum talked for a while. I couldn't hear what they were saying, but I'm guessing he wasn't happy that I was there. Mum must have convinced him I wouldn't get in the way, as I saw him smile before he left. She came over to me and told me that I was not to touch anything or move from where I was sitting.

She then took off her coat and lifted a row of huge bobbins onto a series of spikes on the top of the machine. What happened next took my breath away... She took the thread from one of the bobbins and fed it through every pulley wheel and hook I could see. It's not that she could remember which way to wrap the thread around the pulleys that amazed me... it was the fact that she did it so fast. Her hands were a blur; it was amazing. I lost count of the number of times she did this, because I was hypnotised. After she had loaded the final reel, she flicked a lever and the machine came to life and added another note to the symphony of sound around me. She then turned around to me and smiled as though she had just put the kettle on. When she saw my astonished face, she asked me what was wrong. I just mumbled: "How did you do that?"

I think she suddenly realised that what she thought was just her mundane job was perhaps not so mundane after all. I could see pride fill her face as she said, "I don't think about it... it just happens."

When I said she had hands like rock coated with sandpaper... now I know why. Any normal hands would have been ripped to shreds while loading nylon thread around all those pulleys. If I think about health and safety in the workplace now and compare it to her days... she had no gloves, no ear protectors and no safety guards around the machinery. What a hard way to earn a living.

Most people don't get a chance to see what their parents do for a job, so I feel privileged. I know what a hard life my mother had... I know what she did to ensure that her children had food, clothing and a roof over their heads. I am privileged to have the opportunity to write a book about her, because it allows me to piece together her story. It may not be the complete story, but it's enough to almost create a sort of virtual reality where I can watch her life and appreciate what she did for us.

I'm currently looking at a photo of her when she was a young woman in Italy. I see a woman I never knew. A young, striking and beautiful woman, with her whole life ahead of her. Did she imagine she would travel to England? Did she imagine she would have four children? I'm sure she dreamed of a better life... one without the hardship she experienced as a kid. If she had known that her life in England was to be no easier than her life in Italy, would she have stayed?

I want to reach into the photo and say, "Hi Mum. You look so beautiful. Listen, don't worry about us. Just enjoy your life... you deserve it."

Words of Wisdom: There is wonderment in the seemingly mundane... so just remember that the next time you look at your mum or dad. You don't really know them or what they have been through – or even what they do now.

Chapter 4

Auntie Pina

I feel blessed to have had two Italian mammas in my life; the first, of course, was my mother, but the second was my Auntie Giuseppina, or 'Auntie Pina'. Like my mother, she was the archetypal short, stout and strong Italian mamma. I always remember her dressed in black, with arms folded tightly across her chest. In my mind, I used the word 'breasts', but what I typed was 'chest'. Why? I'll tell you why... Do you know how weird it is to say the word breasts when you're talking about your auntie? Especially this auntie! Even now I'm expecting a clip around the head from her, followed by "You dirty bugger!" OK... risking the clip... I don't think I ever saw her without her arms folded under her breasts. As a kid, I was convinced that her breasts would fall off if she didn't support them. What?! I was a kid... I believed in far weirder stuff than that! I believed that if I played with my belly button, it might burst open and all my insides would flood out... I believed that if I swallowed a watermelon seed, it would germinate inside my stomach and a watermelon plant would start growing out of my bum. Need I go on?

Anyway, back to my description of Auntie Pina. She had short, wavy jet-black hair. I think I remember asking Mum why Auntie Pina's hair was black and hers was going grey. She got a bit angry and said that Auntie Pina got her hair from a bottle... I could never understand how she could get hair into a bottle, never mind get it out of one. What?! I was just a kid!

Auntie Pina had the perfect deep rasping Italian voice, straight out of a gangster movie... well... if it was set in Manchester, that is, because she had just a hint of a Mancunian accent. She would invariably have a stern and disapproving look on her face. The sort of face that said: 'I can see you coming a mile away, so don't give me any of your bullshit.' For those who knew her, this wasn't off-putting at all, because you knew that every now and then, the cold exterior would soften... an eyebrow would be raised... followed closely by that cheeky mischievous smile... her face would light up and, if you were lucky, you would get the giggle.

Pina came from a big family; she had four sisters and one brother. They lived in a small mountain village in the south of Italy called Bivongi. By all accounts she had a tough life, getting up at the crack of dawn each day to spend a full day working in the fields, after which she was expected to do the housework when she got back home. So it wasn't surprising that she followed the stream of Italians who came to England in the 1950s and 1960s in search of a better life.

Why Manchester? It's not the first place on people's lists of dream cities to live, but most of the Italians who moved to the UK did so by being sponsored by a family member or friend. This often meant that small Italian communities would grow in the most unlikely of places, like Manchester,

Glasgow, Bedford and Peterborough. Auntie Pina was sponsored by her elder sister, who was working in a local cotton mill at the time. It must have been such a comfort to know she wasn't going to be all on her own in a foreign country. She had someone to show her the ropes and look after her.

Uncle Armando and Auntie Pina

Her search for a better life began like a dream. She had a job and a place to live and she had her big sister close by. Things would get even better when she met and married my mum's brother Armando. It's strange to think that you can travel hundreds of miles to another country in search of a new life, only to meet and fall in love with someone from back where you started. They came from similar towns in the south of

Italy and similar backgrounds, so there were no cultural differences and no language problems to worry about. Life continued to get better and better as they were blessed with three children: Giuseppe (Zeppie), Christina (Chris) and Giulio (Juju). They bought a house and a car, which was out of reach to many of the people in their work and friendship groups.

They were living the dream... but it wasn't to last. After only six years of marriage and at the unbelievably young age of thirty-one, disaster struck. Armando had a massive and fatal heart attack while walking home one evening. I can only imagine the horror, as Pina's world shattered in an instance. The death of Armando at such a young age left her all on her own, to bring up three young children. Zeppie, at five, was the oldest; Chris was three and Juju was only one. This would have been difficult enough at the best of times, but this wasn't the best of times. Soon after the funeral, the bank repossessed both their home and their car. Pina found herself in a seemingly hopeless situation with no money, nowhere to live and three children to feed. But, like all *Italian mammas*, she had an inner strength... so she rolled up her sleeves and got on with the shitty stick she had been given.

The first priority was to find somewhere to live. Pina was an active member of the local church so she approached them for help, and they allowed her to move into one of their poorhouses. With the relief of having a roof over their heads, now she needed to get a job. She was very fortunate to find work cleaning a doctor's surgery. I say fortunate because, every evening after the surgery had closed, the doctor taught

Auntie Pina how to read and write English. What a wonderful act of kindness and generosity... The world is full of these simple acts of kindness and we should celebrate them.

Auntie Pina's next focus was to get out of the poorhouse and into a home of their own. She was determined to give her children the life they deserved. So, she went out and got two more jobs. This meant she would leave the house early in the morning to start the first of her three jobs. After completing her second job, she would return home to pick the kids up from a neighbour and make them dinner. After dinner was finished, she would go out for her third job and wouldn't be seen again until bedtime. Unfortunately, with all the best intentions, this meant that not only did her children have to live without a father, they effectively had to live without a mother while she worked hard to put food on the table and give them the life that perhaps she never had.

My cousins said that Pina didn't talk much about their dad. This may have been because it hurt to think about him, or it may have been due to an old Italian superstition where they believed that, to ensure the soul of the deceased leaves the earth, they would not only bury them with personal belongings but they would also refrain from talking about them for fear of attracting them back to earth. Tradition also dictates that the widow should wear black for twelve months. I think Auntie Pina may have got months and years mixed up, because all I can ever remember was her wearing black.

She did an amazing job, because I always remember her being financially well off compared to us. All that hard work paid off. What can I say? Another amazingly strong woman who will never be forgotten, because her legacy will live on in the minds and hearts of the people she touched – and now, of course, in print. I asked my cousins what came to mind first when they thought about their mum. They all said: "Her cooking." If you asked a hundred Italians what they think of first when they remember their mothers, I think ninety-nine would say "Her cooking." For Zeppie, Christina and Juju, it was things like: "Pasta and meatballs! Pizza!" Even after they all moved out, they would come home for Sunday lunch and the odd evening meal.

I too remember the pasta and the pizzas, but top of the list for me were her cakes and biscuits. Whenever she came to visit us, she would always bring a sweet surprise. I bless the fact that our eldest daughter experienced this first hand. When Rebecca was very young, we would always pop around to see Auntie Pina when we were up in Manchester. As new parents, we had such high standards of how we were going to bring up our children. No junk food, only home cooked foods, no crisps or biscuits... and we would enforce these rules, because of course we knew best. On one memorable occasion, our resolute rules were quashed by an Italian mamma's raised eyebrow. Soon after we arrived at Auntie Pina's house, she asked Rebecca whether she was hungry, to which we immediately replied: "Oh... she can have a piece of fruit or a carrot." Well, Auntie Pina gave us an unmistakable look... It was the sort of look that said 'You have got to be kidding! You've been parents for two minutes and suddenly you're experts?' Yes... it was definitely that sort of look. She focused the look at me, then at Debbie, then back at me... and then she raised *the eyebrow*. She took Rebecca's hand

and led her to the kitchen. We were a bit suspicious, so we peeked into the kitchen just as she was taking a large tin from the shelf. She offered the contents to Rebecca. The tin swallowed almost all of Rebecca's arm as she rummaged around inside. After a few seconds, with delight on her face, she pulled out a handful of animal cracker biscuits. We then heard Auntie Pina say: "It's our little secret."

After a few minutes, they came out of the kitchen, past us in the living room and went on into the front room. Not even I had been in there! Every Catholic who could afford it would have a room that was 'off bounds' to everyone but 'special' visitors. The ultimate guest would be the local priest, so it had the best furniture and was kept spotless. The kids weren't allowed in there, mainly because she wanted to keep it neat and tidy, but also because it would be too much of a temptation for them. This room was where the alcohol and the special biscuits were kept – and, more importantly, this was where the Christmas and birthday presents were hidden. On this occasion, Rebecca was granted special access. After a few minutes they returned. Auntie Pina was carrying presents for us and Rebecca was beaming, because she was carrying a present for herself.

I miss Auntie Pina so much. I loved her, and I loved visiting her. It was like walking through a magical door into everything Italian. She was our only link to the Italian community. When she came to visit us, she would bring Italian sweets, cakes and pastries. We would eat and drink, then she and Mum would sit on the sofa and talk about how unwell they were. It would start with each of them being polite and faking genuine interest and concern about the other's ailments, but by the end, they were in a no-holds-barred pissing contest. I've never seen two people so determined to have the most excruciatingly painful illness. Then, when they were on the verge of having an argument, Auntie Pina would stand up and say that she had to catch the bus home. There would be hugs, kisses and goodbyes, after which Mum would shut the door and walk off, muttering under her breath, "She's not that ill."

I would have loved for my daughters to have had Auntie Pina in their lives as they grew up, but unfortunately she left us far sooner than she should have, and many years before my mum. At Mum's funeral we joked about what they would be doing up there in heaven. We said they would be arguing with each other to see who had won at being the most ill. Auntie Pina would claim she won because she died first, and Mum would say she had won because she had more things wrong with her and she was in much more pain for far longer. They would reluctantly agree it was a draw, then ask each other if they were hungry. They would smile... and then start complaining about the food in heaven.

I was going to end this chapter here, but I started thinking about my mother's story again. I thought she was unique... She had such a hard life, yet she managed to find the strength to smash her way through adversity. She was a uniquely strong, courageous, selfless and amazingly resilient mamma... but now, I think, not so unique, because I could have used the same description for Auntie Pina.

I then began to wonder whether there was more to this than just two women who had very hard lives and were in possession of a similar strength of character. I wondered whether it had something to do with where they came from. So, I started to look at Italy and its history. It wasn't long before I began to see a common thread in the way the people from the south of Italy were described. It was at this point that I had the pleasure of talking to a lovely lady called Paola Giglio, who is a colleague of my wife. She lives and works in Italy and is especially passionate about the south and its people. She helped me gain a greater understanding of what it is to be from the south and how its history has shaped its culture and its people. She said there is a strong belief that the mother – *la mamma* – was at the heart of Italian family life; it was she who laid down the rules and values that have been absorbed into what is now southern Italian culture. "Family, love, friendship, generosity, hospitality, solidarity, the value of life, feelings and passions were dear to the mamma," she said. So, is it so surprising that the south of Italy could be responsible for blessing the world with *Italian mammas* like my mum and my Auntie Pina?

People who have read my first book *The Leukaemia Diaries* will know that my mind is not wired up like most people's, so please bear with me on this next bit. I have a theory... If I think of a young Italian woman, I will use words like beautiful, confident, hot-headed, liberated and, of course, passionate. On the other hand, when I think of an Italian mamma, I want to use words like strong, courageous and selfless. That's not to say that a mamma cannot be beautiful; it's more that. Their beauty pales into insignificance when compared to their strength and courage.

So, here is the strange bit. I imagine that, when a young

Italian woman decides to become a mother, she goes to sleep one night and enters into a chrysalis state. When she awakens the next morning, she has gone through an amazing transformation and emerges to reveal the ultimate force of nature ...the *Italian mamma*. This same mind then imagines that these women must contain the genetic memory of the trials and tribulations of southern Italy through the ages. This genetic memory arms them with all the knowledge and tools they need to protect, nurture and care for their families.

Rather than just state the existence of genetic memory, the scientist in me wanted to prove it in some way. It came to me while I was watching a wildlife programme that showed how the cuckoo lays an egg in the nest of another species of bird. The egg hatches before the other eggs and the emerging cuckoo chick somehow knows that it must eject all the other eggs from the nest, so it has no competition for food. This isn't instinct; this is the knowledge that it must perform a task to survive. What makes the cuckoo story even more incredible is that it does all this before its eyes are open.

For me, this explains how my mum, Auntie Pina, and all Italian mammas come to share similar values and strength of character. By taking this train of thought even further, this means that the blood that flows through my veins contains the same genetic memory of my mum (and all Italian mammas). If this is the case, then it would be logical to believe that I have passed this on to my children... and it's that thought that makes me proud beyond belief or hope.

Words of Wisdom: Life is, as the song says, "a roller coaster". It's full of ups and downs, twists and turns... love and happiness... joy and sadness... and tears for all occasions. It's easy to get lost in the ride while staring at the tracks ahead. Take time to turn around and look at the people who are in the car with you... and appreciate what you have.

Chapter 5

Superstitions and the Greasy Witch

Growing up in a small mountain village in Italy means you tend to have a unique outlook on life. In particular, you end up having a unique set of superstitions and beliefs. Let's take Mum as an example, shall we? She was very superstitious and made sure we were fully educated and prepared for all of them. I bet you're thinking of the classics, like you'll get bad luck if you walk under a ladder or let a black cat cross your path... or you'll get seven years' bad luck if you smash a mirror?

Well, I grew up with these and many more not so familiar ones. For example, did you know that if you drop a knife, it is bad luck to pick it up yourself? Now, if you live with someone, it's easy enough to ask that someone to pick it up for you, but what if you live on your own? There must be thousands of Italians living on their own without knives, because they're all on the floor! Or... is that why the most popular Italian dish doesn't require a knife to eat? In fact, spaghetti, lasagna, ravioli, risotto... they can all be eaten with a fork!

Did you know it is bad luck to talk while going under a bridge? And did you know it is bad luck to turn a loaf of freshly baked bread upside down? There are also superstitions that I hadn't realised I'd absorbed until I started researching for this book. When I walk hand in hand with my wife and we come up to a lamppost, I insist that we do not break hands and walk either side... in fact, I will get upset if we do. We have to both walk around the same side, while maintaining contact. It turns out that in Italy it is considered bad luck on the friendship to break hands in such a manner.

Some of my favourite superstitions are the ones concerning vampires and witches. Of course, I didn't really know which were common in the UK and which were more unique to Italy. For instance, the first time I brought my wife home to meet Mum, she noticed a pile of rice outside my mum's bedroom door and asked why it was there. I looked at her and said: "You're joking, right?" She shook her head, and I realised that this was one of the superstitions that was unique to Italy, so I explained that the rice was there to keep vampires from entering the bedroom. A vampire would be inextricably drawn to the pile of rice and would have to count every grain before he could enter the bedroom... Of course he would! This would obviously take so long that it would be dawn before he was finished and then he would be hit by sunlight and turn into ash. An upturned broom was used to do the same thing: the vampire would have to count all the bristles. These things really worked, because I can't remember a vampire ever making its way into Mum's bedroom.

Having just written that paragraph, a thought has come to me. She was so obsessed with keeping vampires out of her bedroom but she wasn't bothered about whether they could get into her children's rooms!

Then there is the story I love to tell people of the greasy witch. I bet you were wondering when I was going to get to her. Well, one day Debbie and I were having dinner and chatting about a vampire film we had seen, when Mum slipped something into the conversation. "Don't worry about the future," she said, "because our family is protected for seven generations."

I was used to my mum saying weird things and usually I would just nod or say "Yes," or, to make it sound like I was really listening, I would say "Really?" But on this occasion, I just couldn't let it go. So I said, "What do you mean?" I am so glad I did, because if I didn't, we would all have missed the following 'true' story... and try and remember that this was dramatically delivered by a short stout Italian mamma who truly believed everything she was saying.

She had been out late with a friend, she said, and was walking home. It was a beautiful warm summer's evening and a full moon was illuminating her way... OK, so she wouldn't have said 'illuminating', but this book would be so hard to read if I wrote exactly what she did say. Anyway, she crept into the kitchen so she wouldn't wake anyone, but while cutting a slice of bread for a quick snack she heard some moaning from her father's room upstairs. She thought this was strange because her mother was no longer with them, so he should have been on his own. There was a scream, so naturally she thought something was wrong and rushed upstairs. She burst into his room to find her father in real distress. He had an anguished look on his face, and he was breathing hard and sweating... and on top of him was a greasy witch.

"Whoa... whoa.... stop right there!" I said, when Mum told us the story. "What... how... How did you know she was a witch?"

Mum looked at me as though I'd just put tomato ketchup on my pasta. The look softened a little when she remembered I didn't have the advantage of being born in Italy. Obviously, if I had, I would have grown up with witch folklore. I would have known that, when the moon was full, a young witch would take off all her clothes, smother her naked body with a special oil, then get on her broom and fly out of her window and around the village, looking for a man to seduce. When she found a man, she would cast such a powerful spell over him that he would be unable to resist her.

After composing herself, my mother went on to say that she confronted the witch and pushed her off her dad. She shouted and screamed at the witch to leave her father alone. Apparently, her father tried to defend the witch, to which my mother said: "Don't worry, Papa, I will save you."

She picked up a broom that was in her father's bedroom and used it to push the witch towards the open window. All the time her father was telling Mum to leave the poor girl alone, but Mum said he didn't know what he was saying, because he was obviously still under her spell. Then Mum gave the witch an ultimatum. She pushed her until she was hanging out of the window and said, "If you leave my family for seven generations, I will let you go."

Apparently, the witch was so defenceless that she gave in

and promised to leave our family alone, at which point Mum promptly pushed the witch out of the bedroom window anyway! With pride, she said to us: "So that's why your children and grandchildren will never be bothered by witches."

My mother, the *witch killer*.

I asked her what Nonno had said after she pushed the witch out of the window. She said he thanked her, but she knew he was still under her spell, because he kept looking out of the window. She then said: "I put a pair of scissors on his windowsill to keep her away and in the morning he was better." Apparently, witches are scared of metal objects! All I could think about was the poor girl, who was obviously having an affair with my Nonno. One second she was having a wonderful time, and the next she was being pushed out of a first storey bedroom window... naked.

As I said, my mother truly believed this actually happened. She believed that a witch had flown in through the bedroom window and seduced her father. Debbie and I just chuckled to ourselves. We have recounted this story many times, and each time I laugh at how my mum could truly have believed in such ridiculous folklore.

Well... my laughter subsided a little when I did some research on witches before writing this chapter. And I must admit I found it very interesting. I talked to a number of people who had an interest in folklore and came across several stories that described how, on the evening of a full moon, witches would coat their brooms with a special 'flying ointment' before flying out into the night. These stories said the flying ointment needed to be ingested by the witches in order to enable them to fly. The problem was they couldn't swallow the ointment, because it would make them sick. So, it had to be absorbed into the body via another route. These other routes, apparently, were places like the vagina and anus. Hence why they anointed the broom and flew naked. Anyway. Once airborne, they would seek out an unsuspecting male and put a spell on him, so they could have their wicked way with him... Something makes me think that all they really needed to do was ask and they would be just as successful. Let's look at that scenario... naked witch flies into your room and asks for sex... mmm... let me think.

I also discovered that there was a hot spot for witchcraft just a few miles away from where my mother grew up, in a place called Benevento. The witches from Benevento were also able to transform into a mist and gain entry to a house through the gap under the door... and yes, you guessed it, some of the ways to stop witches coming in were to place various objects near the door or window, like an upturned broom, a pile of salt or a piece of iron... a pair of scissors, perhaps?

I'll leave you with one last thought, something that niggled at me after I had written the story down. Why did my Nonno have a broom in his bedroom?

Words of Wisdom: Always make sure you have a supply of salt, rice, iron and brooms.

Chapter 6

Don't Come Running to Me If You Break Both Your Legs!

Although Mum had been in the UK for many years, she never quite got to grips with the local sayings. For instance, there's the classic 'Don't come running to me if you break both your legs,' used by parents who have warned their children about the dangers of doing something, to no avail. No kid could ever understand this saying. The first time they heard it, they would turn around and say: "How can I come running if my legs are broken?" and, after uttering this wise analysis, would get a clip around the ear for their back chat. Mum used this phrase quite a lot, but her version was much more alarming and, if anything, more sensible. She would say: "Come running to me and I'll break both your legs!" She would always get the attention of other parents when she shouted this down the street and all the kids would look at me with genuine fear on their faces.

When a kid had done something wrong and was being interrogated by their parents, the parent would ask: "Why did you do it?" and the kid would often respond, "Because my mates were all doing it." This invoked the classic parental response, "If all your friends jumped off a bridge, would you?" to which you were not expected to reply. Mum's version of this was short and straight to the point, because she would just say: "Jump off a bridge." When I pointed out that she wasn't saying it right, she clipped me around the ear and said, "Don't chatty your back to me." And when I said that wasn't right either, she then shouted something in Italian. Well, of course, I found this funny and started to chuckle, to which the normal parental response would be "You'd better wipe that smile off your face or I'll wipe it off for you." But Mum would say: "Do you want me to wipe your face?"

As a kid, I would always push people just that one step too far. Some would say I am quick-witted; others would say I have no filter – and if you'd met my mum, you'd probably say I had a death wish. I used to do that thing where I could turn my eyelids inside out. It would freak her out and she would mean to shout, "If you keep making that face and the wind changes, it'll freeze that way." But what she actually said was: "The wind will freeze your face like that." Which, compared to the other phrases, is pretty good, but that suicidal wit of mine would respond with: "Is that what happened to your face?" I think you can guess what happened next.

Back to the phrase about breaking both my legs. That was used quite a lot, partly because she was a typical over-protective Italian mother and partly because I was good at getting into trouble. The list is endless, but let's start with the Bionic Man. We used to live opposite a huge woodyard, which was the most amazing place to play around in as a kid. Obviously, we weren't allowed to be in there and in retrospect it was a dangerous place to have as your playground, but the lure was just irresistible.

I remember my friend and I had sneaked under the gates one Sunday when the yard was closed. It was a precision operation, because we had to wait until the security guard had passed on his regular rounds. Then we ran to the very centre of the woodyard. Just to give you an idea of what this place was like, it was probably the size of two football pitches and packed with rows and rows of wood. They were mostly long planks stacked to various heights; some of the stacks would be taller than a house. The security guard never patrolled the centre, so we could play there for hours without fear of being caught.

On that particular day, we were climbing on one of the tallest wood stacks when I had a great idea... well, I thought it was great. At the time there was a TV programme called *The Six Million Dollar Man*. He was a test pilot who had a near fatal crash, but he was saved by some specialist surgeon who gave him two bionic legs, a bionic arm and a bionic eye. It meant he could jump really high, bend iron bars and see for miles. Whenever he did one of his jumps, it would always be shown in slow motion and with sound effects. My great idea was to climb to the top of the highest wood stack and jump down to one of the lower stacks. It was probably about a ten metre drop... I told you it was a great idea! I told my friend and he too thought it was a great idea, although he thought I would never do it, because it was impossible. Impossible?... "Ha! They have stunt men doing all the jumps, so how difficult can it be?" I said.

He kept goading me and saying I was too chicken to do it. Well, not only did I say I was going to do it, but that I was going to do it right there and then. I asked him to go to the lower wood stack and make the sound effects as I jumped down. I can hear you all saying, "What a stupid idea. You are going to hurt yourself." Where were you forty-five years ago? I could have done with that advice then. Anyway, in my eleven-year-old head, I thought it would be the coolest thing to do and it would be talked about by everyone at school. As I shouted down to my friend that I was ready to jump, I still didn't think it was a bad idea... After all, if Lee Majors could do it, then I could do it, couldn't I?

My friend gave me the countdown. "Three... two... one... jump!" And, obediently and without hesitation or fear, I jumped.

My friend said it was the most amazing thing he had ever seen, better than some of the jumps the Bionic Man had done. He'd forgotten to do the sound effects, because he couldn't help but stare as I flew through the air. He had never seen anyone's legs bend the way mine did as I landed on the lower wood stack. He said he couldn't wait to tell everyone at school... and, as the ambulance doors were being closed, I heard him say he would ask his mum if he could come and visit me in hospital.

After a few weeks off school I was able to walk again, so I asked Mum if I could go out and play with my friend. She warned me to stay away from the woodyard. I said we were just going to catch butterflies with our fishing nets. She told me not to run about, because my ankles were very weak, and that if I didn't listen to her... then I shouldn't come running back to her otherwise she would break both my legs.

So, my friend and I got our fishing nets, an apple and some string, then made our way to the woodyard. What?... We weren't going there to climb. We were going there to re-enact a famous historical event. While I was off school I had watched loads of films on TV. It wasn't like today, where you could choose what you wanted to watch from an endless list. No, we only had three channels, so there wasn't a lot of choice, but every afternoon there would be a matinee film. It was usually an old black and white movie, but I used to look forward to them. One particular film gave me a great idea. It was about William Tell and how he had shot an apple off his son's head with a bow and arrow. So, I told my friend about the film, and that I had a great idea. My idea was that we should make bows out of our fishing nets and shoot apples off each other's heads. He thought it was a fantastic idea. What do you mean it was a stupid idea? Well... it's a bit bloody late to tell me that now!

Anyway, when we got to our favourite spot in the middle of the woodyard, we set about converting the fishing nets into bows and arrows. Now, when I say fishing net, it was only a long piece of bamboo with a small net stuck in the end. We used to go fishing with them for newts and sticklebacks in the local canal. We pulled the net off and then cut the bamboo into two pieces. One of the pieces was twice as long as the other, so one was for the bow and the other was for the arrow. It took us a while because we had to use my friend's dad's Swiss Army knife, which had one of those saw blades. We cut slits at either end of the longer bit and tied a piece of string on one end. We then bent the stick as much as we dared and tied off the string on the other end to make the bow. With the smaller piece, we sharpened one end with the knife and then tied some pigeon feathers to the other end to make the arrow.

We each had a bow and one arrow, and they worked brilliantly. In the film, the father asks the son to stand against a tree. He walks twenty paces away from the tree, then turns and shoots the apple off his son's head. I told my friend he could go first. I stood against one of the wood stacks and put the apple on my head. He walked twenty paces, turned quickly and shot his arrow at the apple. It was a bit of an anti-climax, as the arrow landed at my feet. We laughed and decided perhaps we should make it fifteen paces. It was my turn, so my friend assumed the position with the apple on his head and I walked the fifteen paces. As I was walking, I thought I would have to fire my arrow a lot harder than he did in order to hit the apple. So, when I turned, I made sure I pulled the arrow as far back as it could, then... "Twang!"... and the arrow was released. It shot out of my bow like a... well, like an arrow. I could see the arrow was on target, and I remember getting excited and thinking that it was going to be perfect... I was going to hit the apple with my first shot. They wouldn't believe this at school when we told them on Monday. Then the arrow hit its target, but unfortunately it wasn't the apple... It hit my friend straight between his eyes. I immediately ran over to him, shouting about how amazing it was. The arrow had glided perfectly through the air and it only just missed the apple. People at school would be amazed by this one! And, as the ambulance doors closed, I also said I would ask my mum if I could visit him in hospital... (*Don't worry, he was fine – just a scar –*

but it could have been so much worse.)

Our parents agreed that when my friend came out of hospital, we shouldn't play with each other anymore and we were both forbidden to play in the woodyard. Which, of course, meant that we had to go to the woodyard separately from then on. What?!

We agreed to wait a week before we got together, which gave me a lot of time to think. So when we met up in the woodyard I told him that I had another great idea... No!... This was my best one yet. I had watched an old black and white film about a bunch of kids who built a go-kart from offcuts of wood and an old pram.

It took us a few trips to the local tip to scavenge the bits we needed. Then we had to take all the bits to another friend's backyard to build the go-kart, because we couldn't be seen together. My friend had liberated his dad's tools and we were off! We worked late that night and most of the next morning, but by lunchtime it was ready. Our go-kart was brilliant, even if I do say so myself. It had seating big enough for two, it could be steered with the feet or by a thick piece of rope connected to the front axle and it glided on the tarmacked roads. The only thing left to do was a test ride.

We had agreed that the only place it could be tested properly was down Widow's Peak. Now, before you get carried away, nobody had ever died on Widow's Peak; it was just a very steep hill. It was only about 400 metres long, but it was very steep and at the end was a T-junction where it met a quiet road. Across the T-junction was an old walled garden with a big wooden gate that was always open. So, the plan was that we would drive the go-kart down the hill faster than anyone had ever been before and at the bottom we would cross the road and then go straight through the gate and into the garden. The garden was full of soft earth and luscious plants, so it would be the ideal place to crash... not that we were going to crash.

When we got to the top of Widow's Peak we had a crowd of adoring fans to support us... well, a few mates who wanted to watch us crash. It was the perfect day for it. The sun was shining, there was no wind and our parents were at work. Perfect. We both got in, me at the front and my friend behind. I took a tight hold of the steering rope and put my feet firmly on the front axle. We were ready. Another friend gave the countdown... three... two... one...go! And he gave us an almighty push – in fact, he kept pushing us until he could no longer keep up. It was a much faster start than I had anticipated. By the time we were halfway down the hill, we were going so fast I could hardly keep my eyes open because the air was hurting them.

It was at this point that I remembered what was missing from the go-kart design... BRAKES! It was a slight oversight, I know, but I guess we didn't think we would ever reach such speeds. We just seemed to get faster and faster. The go-kart was now starting to become difficult to control. I had to concentrate really hard to keep it in a straight line so we could safely cross the T-junction and go into the garden opposite.

As we got close to the T-junction there were two things we noticed. The first was that there were several cars coming along the usually empty road. And secondly, the gate to the garden was shut. I'm not sure which scared us most. I felt my co-driver grip my shoulders tightly and shout: "Cars!... Stop!... Stop!" When I politely told him we had no breaks he freaked out. "We're gonna die!" he said... shouted... no, it was more of a high-pitched scream. I tried putting my feet on the floor to slow us down, but it made hardly any difference. Before we knew it, we were at the road and heading straight for the rear of a passing car... which we missed by a whisker. We went from certain death to utter relief in the blink of an eye. Then the eye blinked again and we went back to certain death as we hurtled towards the closed garden gate. Then I remember closing my eyes...

There was a big thud. The next thing I remember was my head throbbing, my hands bleeding and my friend sitting in a bed of stinging nettles. He turned to me and asked: "Do you think we'll go to the same hospital?"

Fortunately, we didn't need to go to hospital; in fact, we walked away with just a few scratches and bruises. The go-kart was a write-off, but at least we did it and we had witnesses, which was the most important thing. We were elated afterwards, because for a short period of time we were cool... well, coolish. Until, that is, one of our neighbours told our parents what had happened. We both got a good slap and were grounded for the next few weeks. We were told never to play with each other again... and this time they really meant it.

Indestructible me

When Debbie read this chapter, she said she could see that young boy in the man she married. She said the boy was fearless. He didn't waste time worrying about whether he would fail or get hurt; he just jumped in with two feet. He was indestructible. He was a dreamer... and he believed he was a super hero.

The more I thought about it, the more I could see it. As a kid, I loved to watch films on TV, particularly sci-fi and fantasy. Each film I watched would give me a couple of hours where I would be sucked into the world they created. I would often recreate these worlds in the front room of our house. I would shut the curtains, turn out the lights and sit in an armchair, which would miraculously become the seat of my spaceship. I would put a ruler down the side of the seat cushion, and this would be the throttle. Five, four, three, two, one... Blast off! I would be hurtling through the universe, battling evil space creatures and rescuing shipmates. This would go on for hours, and I would see less and less of the front room and more and more of the world I had created in my mind. So, you can imagine what a shock it was when I was dragged, kicking and screaming, back to the real world when the front door opened and in walked Mum to shatter the illusion. I am sure this is where my vivid imagination and romanticism was born and perfected. Yes, romanticism... a film couldn't just have the spaceships or the fantasy monsters, it also had to have a romantic or inspirational strand to it.

I am just the same today. I love to watch sci-fi and fantasy films, where I will immerse myself in the worlds they create. The romantic in me will always be looking for the *Star Trek* moment: you know, that moment in a film where a character says something so inspiring it brings a tear to your eye. In the 2009 *Star Trek* film, Christopher Pike says to the young Jim Kirk, "You know, your father was captain of a starship for twelve minutes. He saved 800 lives – including your mother's and yours. I dare you to do better."

Perhaps only sci-fi geeks will get that one, but every good film has a *Star Trek* moment. Even everyday life has *Star Trek* moments... you just have to look for them.

Words of Wisdom: When someone says they have a great idea, run away! But make sure you don't miss the Star Trek *moments in life.*

Chapter 7

If the Rats and the Cockroaches Don't Get You, the Killer Rabbit Will

The first house I remember living in was that classic 'two up, two down' mid-terraced council house we moved into after Mum's divorce. It was the sort of house you see in old television footage from the north of England in the 50s and 60s: rows and rows of red-brick terraced houses as far as the eye could see... well, as far as a young kid could see. Every house was the same, with a front door that led straight into the living room, where the settee and television would be. Another door opposite the front door led into the kitchen. Once in the kitchen, there would be another door directly opposite that led into the backyard. This backyard was about three metres wide and two metres long and the ground was covered in huge stone slabs. There wasn't much room at all, especially since about a third of the space was taken up by an outside toilet and a shed.

Across the yard, and directly opposite the kitchen door, was a large wooden gate that led on to the 'ginnel'. Yes, ginnel... not alleyway, passageway or snicket, no... it was a ginnel. The ginnel separated the backyards of one whole street of houses from the backyards of the houses in the street behind. It was a place where I often used to play when

I was young. For such a seemingly uninteresting place, it managed to keep my attention for hours, mainly because of the wildlife that lived there. It makes me chuckle now when my youngest daughter comes running to tell me there is a huge spider in her bedroom. I dutifully follow her to see the giant monster that has been terrorising her, knowing it will be tiny. I want to say, "Call that a spider?" and take her back in time to the ginnel of my youth, where I'd point at the prehistoric monsters crawling around the walls and say: "Now that's a spider!"

It wasn't just that they were huge. They had thick hairy legs and they weren't scared of little boys – or scared of anything, for that matter. I used to watch the battles that went on in their webs. There was the 'no contest' bar snack, which was the greenfly... fairly boring. Then there were the starters, the bluebottles and house flies, that put up a bit more of a fight and certainly made more noise. The main meal was the more exciting battles with wasps and bees; the spiders would certainly know they had been in a fight. Dessert was a caterpillar, an easy fight, but fattening. So, as you can see, I would be entertained for hours during the day.

At night, the ginnel was the domain of the cats and the rats. Now I think about it, I have no memories of cats in the streets during the day. I only remember them at night. I also remember they would always be up on the walls, because the rats ruled the ground. I don't think I ever saw a cat chasing or killing a rat, mainly because there were too many of them and they were huge. The cats mainly fought each other... and they did it very loudly, all night long.

A standard night would start slowly, with the sound of

babies crying... at least, that's what it sounded like. In actual fact, it was the cats slowly picking fights with each other. Perhaps they were jostling for the best places on the walls. This would go on for a while but slowly got louder and more intense. There would come a point where you knew the screeching couldn't get any louder and all hell would break loose. You could tell they had finally come to blows when the screeching became deep and erratic. It lasted for ten or twenty seconds and would always be followed by a loud noise and then silence. I presumed the cats had fallen off the wall while scratching chunks out of each other. They usually landed on a dustbin and, because dustbins in those days were made of metal, there would be a huge clattering as they fell over. After the clatter, the cats would be silent, because they suddenly realised where they were... in the domain of the rats! The next thing to happen – or, more accurately, the next sound – would come from the cats as they started screeching again. This new screeching was more desperate, as I suspected that both cats were probably being attacked by the rats.

There would be a lull in the wall top activity, and then the whole thing started again. You could look out of the back-bedroom window and see silhouettes of twenty or thirty cats along the brick walls. Each bunch of silhouettes would take their turn at having a 'cat scrap'. At some point during this feline rave, a bedroom light would expose them, mid-fight. What seemed like hundreds of reflective cats' eyes froze as if, in doing so, they were invisible to the unwanted intruder. A sash window would open, a voice would scream, "Will you shut the fuck up! I've got work in the morning!"

and an object would come flying out of the window and hit the nearest cat. After that, all but the bravest cats vanished into the darkness.

Like the cats, there was no way any human wanted to be out in the backyard at night, but, unfortunately, the only household toilet was out there. When you were very young you could use the potty under the bed to relieve yourself, but as you got older that wasn't an option... especially if you were sharing a bed with two brothers, as I did. So, if you couldn't hold it in until morning, you had to get the emergency toilet pack. "What's in the emergency toilet pack?" I hear you asking. Well, I'm surprised you don't know. So, for the uninitiated, the pack contained: a box of matches, a pile of what we called 'dilemma newspaper' ripped into squares, and a hammer. What, you want me to explain? OK... Just to set the scene, there were no lights in the backyard and it would invariably be cold and very dark. You had to make sure you were really prepared before you opened the back door. Shoes? Check. Coat? Check. Emergency toilet pack? Check. Only when you had three checks would you even contemplate unlocking the back door.

Once the door was unlocked, the next step only lasted a couple of seconds; any longer could spell disaster. You would fling open the door, jump out and pull the door shut behind you. That door had to be closed as quickly as possible, otherwise the rats would rush in. After successfully closing the door, you would swivel and take one big stride towards the toilet door... kick open the door and bang the wall with the hammer. You had to be careful not to block the door opening, because the rats didn't like to be cornered and would attack. So, if there was no movement inside the toilet, you would jump in and shut the door. The next step had to happen quickly as well... take a few pieces of the dilemma newspaper, scrunch them up on the floor near the closed door and set light to them using the matches. "Why was it called 'dilemma newspaper'?" I hear you ask... I'll come to that in a minute. The fire near the door was to keep the rats out. There was only a very small gap underneath the door but believe me when I say that even the biggest of rats could squeeze themselves under the smallest of gaps.

So, you're in the toilet, the door is shut, and the fire is lit. You have to let your eyes adjust to the light and then double check there are no rats in there. Now, the next bit requires faith. Why faith? Well, in those days outdoor toilets may have looked like normal toilets, but they most definitely were not. When you lifted the toilet seat, instead of seeing the bottom of the toilet with some water in it you would see a two- or three-metre drop directly into the flowing sewer beneath. So the act of faith was hoping that the rats you could see in the sewer below couldn't make their way up the toilet while you were sitting on it! Once you were on the toilet you had to be quick, because you didn't have a lot of dilemma paper for the fire, and the fire was the only thing keeping the rats out. But the dilemma paper was also your toilet paper... The reason it was called 'dilemma paper' was because you always ended up with the same dilemma: do I use more paper for the fire and hope I have enough left to clean up? The hammer was there to help with the dilemma; well, in principle it was... In principle, when the fire went out

72

and the rats started squeezing under the door you could hit them with the hammer. The only problem was that when the fire went out it was dark and all you could see were shadows blocking the light from the kitchen window, so you could never guarantee that a rat didn't sneak in. Anyway, after the successful completion of your mission, you had to repeat the exercise in reverse... And you wonder why I never forgot it.

I have had many rat experiences in my life, but the one that sealed my pathological fear and hatred of them happened when I was about 10 years old. I was playing 'down th' ginnel' with a friend, when we noticed one of the backyard doors was slightly open. We knew the house had been unoccupied for a while and we'd been daring each other to go into it, because there was a rumour going around that the owners had been killed and were now haunting the house. (Of course, no one had been killed, but kids are great at making up scary rumours.) Anyway, on this particular day we plucked up enough courage to go and check it out. We stood outside the gate for ages before we actually pushed it open. It made the classic scary creaking noise, as all doors in a scary story should make... it's the law.

The yard was empty, apart from the compulsory tin bath leaning up against the wall. We tried to look through the window into the kitchen but it was fairly high, and it was dark inside, so we couldn't see much. My mate tried the back door... and it was open! Shit... that meant we had to go in. Now we were shitting ourselves. It's one thing to snoop around the backyard, but it's an altogether different thing to actually go into the haunted house. What? Of course it was haunted! Why would Dave from number 82 lie about something like that?!

After daring each other for five minutes, we opened the door. It was dark and really smelly. There was an oppressive atmosphere in there, which really started to make me shiver. With every step into the kitchen our eyes got more accustomed to the light, and with every step we started to see more detail of the inside of the house. The next bit happened so quickly and was one of the most rigidly frightening moments of my life. My mate shouted: "What the fuck is that?! What the fuck...! The floor is moving! Shit... the floor is moving!"

There was an eerie silence for a few seconds. Then we both yelled the same word at the same time: "Rats!" Screaming, we ran from the kitchen into the backyard, closely followed by hundreds of rats... well, it was probably more like six or seven. We hit the opening to the back gate at the same time and wedged each other tight, whereupon our human compassion came to the surface... and yes, you guessed it, it was every man for himself as we each tried to drag the other back. Once we were through the gate, we ran... and ran... and ran... I don't think we stopped until we got to the local secondary school, which was at least 10 minutes away. It still brings a shiver to my spine... I hate rats!

As the ground outside was the domain of the rats, then you could say that the ground floor inside the house was the domain of ...the cockroaches. Oh yes, cockroaches! When I was young there would be times when my asthma was so bad, my mum would set up a bed downstairs for me. She did this because normally I had to share a bed with my two brothers, and I would just keep them up all night when I was bad. She also thought it would help me relax. Well, that's what she thought, but the reality was something out of a creepy horror movie.

She would make up a nice comfy bed for me on the sofa and, after my brothers and sister went to bed, she would rub some Vicks decongestant on my chest, give me my inhaler and go upstairs to her own bed. Before she left the room, she would switch off the light. I would always beg her to leave it on, but she would say, "Don't be silly," and carry on upstairs, closing the kitchen door behind her.

Darkness would engulf the room. As I sunk slowly beneath my blanket, I would reach down to the floor and pick up one of my shoes. I could hear the creaking as Mum made her way up the stairs, across the ceiling and into bed. There would be some muffled conversation as she talked to my sister, who slept in the same bed as her, then silence.

As the human shift settled down to sleep, the night life started to stir. It began slowly at first, but as the night shift became confident that the ground floor was theirs, they became bolder. Unseen creatures would scratch and make noises all around me. These old houses had cheap polystyrene ceiling tiles in every room. They were seen as a good way to freshen up the rooms while adding a bit of heat insulation, but the big problem with them was that cockroaches loved them. They slept between the tiles and the ceiling during the day, and at night they would scratch their way out to feed and increase their population. The noise they made was so loud, it sounded like there were thousands of them – which was obviously an exaggeration, because there were only hundreds!

So there I am, with just my face peeping out from beneath the blanket, eyes wide open, flinching every time there was movement close by. When it got too much to bear, I would jump from my makeshift bed in the direction of the light switch on the wall. My first step would always result in a crunching sound as I stepped on an unseen intruder. As soon as the light was on, it was like the discovery of a mass break out at a prison... cockroaches scrambling in every direction, seeking the refuge of the nearest crack or crevice. My vegan daughters would probably frown at me for this, but I took the opportunity to smash as many cockroaches as I could with the heel of my shoe. I held it in my right hand like a hammer and for the first few seconds I was spoilt for targets, but after ten or fifteen seconds the opportunities got fewer and fewer, until it was just the stragglers, who kept changing direction so as not to present an easy target. Unfortunately for them they were doing this in circles, so they never really got very far, and I would finish these stragglers off, then compose myself for round two.

I would turn the light out and remain still, just for a few seconds, because cockroaches have the shortest memory in the insect world and would forget what happened last time the lights went out. I waited until I could hear a lot of activity, then on went the light and down came the heel of justice... splat.... thump... splat! "What are you doing?" came the muffled cry from my mum upstairs, and she would stamp hard on the bedroom floor, which dislodged a cockroach who thought he was being smart by crawling across the ceiling tiles... Splat!

This would go on for ages, either until the numbers finally started to dwindle or I was so knackered that I couldn't do it anymore. The carpet would look like a battlefield, with dead bodies everywhere... or so I thought (the dead bit). Because after a few minutes, these so-called dead bodies would start to move. The odd twitch at first, then more frantic movement until one out of five would burst into life and make a new bid for freedom. Do you ever remember those funny news stories about how some university had spent five years researching cockroaches and had come to the conclusion that they could survive a nuclear holocaust? Well, I totally believe it... they are bloody indestructible!

But there is a knack to killing a cockroach. A carpet is not the best place to try and kill them, because they just get squashed into the spongy surface. You have to follow the splat with a dig and twist! It's extra effort, but it does mean you don't have to kill them twice. It's funny, but all that activity would normally take my mind off my asthma and I would generally have a great night's sleep.

Returning to the backyard and the dominance of the rats at night. The frantic midnight trips to the toilet became the norm and were treated much as any other chore – only to be interrupted for a few glorious months. Those few months coincided with my mum bringing home a giant black rabbit. Apparently, it belonged to a neighbour, but it had grown bigger than they expected and they no longer had any room for it. Well, that was the story they told my mum. The real reason was soon to become apparent.

Mum took the box containing the cuddly ball of fluff into the backyard and we all lined up behind her, excited to see our new pet. She placed the box on the floor and opened the flaps, and two huge black bunny ears popped out. There was a yelp of excitement from my sister and Mum immediately said: "Shhhh! He's scared." She turned back to the box and opened the remaining flaps and now a head popped out, nose twitching and eyes blinking. I'm sure the rabbit was wondering where it was and who these strange people were. Mum asked: "Who wants to stroke it?"

I immediately jumped in and said: "Me... Me... Me!" At which point the cute fluffy little rabbit turned into the Hound of the Baskervilles. Its red eyes – yes, red! – looked evil and full of unpleasant intent. It jumped out of the box with the intention of ripping my face off. No... I am not exaggerating! It sunk its huge vampire teeth into my hand... the hand, I may point out, that was protecting my face. I screamed, turned to run, bumped into my sister and fell to the floor. Then time seemed to slow down...

The rabbit was sitting in the middle of the backyard, my sister and I were on the floor, my two brothers were close to the kitchen door and Mum was behind the rabbit. You could see it was thinking it was free... and there was new meat to attack. After planning its next move, it pounced and bit the nearest thing at hand, which was my sister. Then it went for each of my brothers in turn, taking big lumps out of their ankles. This evil spawn from hell wanted to kill anything in its sight, so we tried as quickly as humanly possible to get the hell out of that sight. After we had all managed to get through the kitchen door and slam it behind us, we assessed the damage. No one was free of scratches, teeth marks or blood. We burst out laughing... Now we knew why our dear neighbour really got rid of the rabbit.

For the next few days until Mum got the hutch from the kind neighbour, the backyard became a 'no go' area. When the hutch finally appeared, it had a new thick wire mesh door on the front. I suspect the rabbit had ripped his way through the old one in one of his mad rages. Anyway, once the hutch was in place, he was allowed a few hours a day to roam around the yard. The rest of the time he was locked safely away.

Mum was the only one who could handle the rabbit. They had come to an understanding, after Mum got angry when he bit her on the breast. She grabbed him by the ears and bit him back and he was so shocked, he never touched her again. To everyone else he was the mad killer rabbit and we all stayed out of his way. Even the rats were scared of him... so much so that for three glorious months I could go to the toilet at night without fear. It was brilliant – and well worth putting up with a killer rabbit for.

But, like all good things, it didn't last. One day, I came home from school and he was gone. Mum said he had bitten through the wood of his hutch and escaped through the back gate and down the ginnel. I was sort of sad to see him go, not because I liked him, but because now I had to go back to the emergency toilet packs. I wasn't sad for too long though, because that night we had lamb for dinner... well, it tasted like lamb.

Words of Wisdom: It's easy to think everything in your life is bad or going wrong... but just remember that every now and then you get to go to the toilet without being attacked by rats.

Chapter 8

The Loan Shark

Like most people in our neighbourhood, my mother regularly used loan sharks, or money lenders. She generally used them on the run up to Christmas, to buy presents and food, and then spent the rest of the year paying off the debt. Much later, I was shocked to learn that if she borrowed something like a hundred pounds from a loan shark, she would often end up paying three hundred back. It's disgusting to think that there are individuals who will take advantage of poor people like my mother and bleed them dry. They would loan people money during a difficult time, then charge them so much in interest that they would be paying it back forever. Then, just as they paid off the loan, they would have to take out another loan.

In those days, you couldn't arrange it over the phone or on the internet; it was all done face to face. When you wanted a loan, you didn't even have to go to their office... more likely you never knew where their office was, or even if they had one. All you had to do was stop the guy in the street and tell them how much you wanted to borrow, because everyone in our neighbourhood used him, so he was easy to find. Later that week, there would be a knock at the door. He and my mother would go into the kitchen. The door would close and there would be a muffled conversation, not loud enough for us to discern what was said. Of course, at the time I didn't know who he was or what was going on. I just knew that, for a while after his visit, things would be great. For a wonderfully short time, my mother would be happy. That night, we would have fish and chips for tea (or dinner, as I call it now, because I is posh now), with a nice piece of cake for pudding.

The next day, she would take us down to the market to buy new clothes or shoes. She would buy more food than we'd seen for months and we would stuff our faces like there was no tomorrow. Mum would go off to bingo for three or four nights in a row and she would always come back with fish and chips and bottles of dandelion and burdock. This would go on until the week after Christmas and then the mood would start to change, because now she had to start paying back the loan. I think the reason she went to bingo so much was because she hoped she would win enough money to pay off the loan, but it rarely happened.

Once a loan had been taken out, you then joined the 'Friday night ritual'. Every Friday afternoon you could look down the long, cobbled streets of Manchester and see children playing outside their houses. The noise was of children screaming, shouting, laughing and crying. The sounds and sights of my childhood. As afternoon turned into early evening, the sounds would slowly subside as the children were called in by their mothers. Then, in the distance, the money collector would start his rounds. He was smartly dressed in suit, tie and long dark overcoat. Armed with his brown book, he'd go from door to door collecting money, ticking boxes next to names to show they had paid, or putting a cross to indicate they had missed a week. His brown book contained all the loan and repayment details of hundreds of people in our area. He had a big black leather satchel containing hundreds of pounds in loose change... Well, that's what the kids believed was in there. You could hear the jingling of loose coins from his money bag long before you ever saw him. We kids didn't know he was a loan shark; we all thought he was the rent man, probably because he knocked on most of the doors in our street.

As he knocked on each door, you would hear raised voices. Then, generally, a child would answer the door and you would hear the man say: "Is your mother in?" When he came to our door, my mum would never let us see her pay him. It was always a secretive affair. She would even try and hide it from the neighbours, which was ridiculous considering he had been to most of them that evening.

Skipping one week's payment was fairly common, and Mum would often get us to answer the door and tell him, "Mum said she'll pay you double next week." He was used to it, so it wasn't a problem, and he would just write in his book and go off to the next house. Missing two weeks was a different story and was very much frowned upon. I remember there was a definite change in protocol when Mum was going to miss a second week's payment.

She would call us in early on a Friday, so we could have our evening meal early. That way, we could finish up and turn off the TV and the lights and hide in the kitchen for a while, pretending not to be at home when the loan shark knocked. I'm sure he knew we were hiding... I'm sure it happened all the time. Things would be back to normal when she paid double the next week and promised to do the same the week after.

Skipping three weeks was almost never done and was seen as a big deal. I remember one occasion when my shoes had finally fallen to pieces and I had nothing to wear to school. When I told Mum, she was mad and went off on one of her classic Italian rants. It was like the world had ended. Back then, I couldn't understand why she was so mad, but what I didn't realise was that she had already missed two weeks' payments for the loan shark and she knew she would have to use this week's money to buy me new shoes. She must have been so unbelievably scared and worried. What was she going to do? That Friday, we were out playing on the street as normal when Mum called us in early. I guessed that it was an early meal night, followed by the whole family hiding in the kitchen until the loan shark had passed.

We went in as planned. Mum had made pasta with cheese and was dishing it out to my eldest brother Mike when my little sister Diane and I came in. I got my pasta, sat down next to my brother Chris and started to tuck in. Mike had just gone back into the kitchen when there was a knock at the door. He came out of the kitchen with a bowl of pasta in one hand and fork in his mouth. Casually, he walked to the door and opened it. I looked up and his face went pale. "Mum... Mum!" he shouted.

There was an annoyed grunt from the kitchen and Mum came into the front room. "What do you want?" she asked. Mike stepped away from the door to reveal the loan shark. Mum just stood there with her mouth open, like a rabbit in the headlights of a car.

The loan shark wasn't supposed to be here... he was far too early. Mum just couldn't understand why he was there so early. Unfortunately, that was an unusual day, because just about everyone on our street had decided to miss their payment this week, which meant he had reached our house at least thirty minutes earlier than normal. After what seemed like an eternity, Mum suddenly said: "Why are you here?"

The loan shark looked puzzled. "To pick up this week's payment?" Mum responded by saying she had paid double last week. Well, everyone in the room knew that wasn't true. The debt collector went through the motions of checking his book and then said: "Erm... no you didn't, Mrs Hyde."

Well, that set off the firework that was my mother! She went ballistic and started shouting and screaming. "Oh my God! Oh my God! I paid... I paid!" Grabbing her hair tightly with both hands, she started to circle the front room, chanting: "Oh my God! I paid... You wanna killa me! Killa me! Oh my God!" She ended up in front of the TV, looking out over her four children, who were sitting on the sofa watching telly while they ate their food. Behind the sofa, the loan shark, with his opened book, was just staring at this mad Italian woman.

Mum then decided to take things to another level. "Oh my God... Oh my God!" she shouted, before collapsing gracefully and with amazing precision on the floor in front of the fireplace. I say amazing precision, because she managed to miss all our feet and the sharp fire surround and fall with her arm conveniently and comfortably under her head. After

85

she had landed on the floor, time seemed to stop for a few seconds. With our mouths full of pasta, we just looked at each other, then looked down at Mum, then back at each other. Then time started again, and we went back to watching the TV.

The loan shark was so shocked and embarrassed that the only thing he could do was say "Mrs Hyde...? Mrs Hyde...? I think I'll come back next week... No need to see me out, Mrs Hyde... I'll be off then, Mrs Hyde." Slowly, he edged his way to the front door, opened it and left quietly. Once again, time stood still. We all looked at each other, then at Mum... then back at the TV.

She was motionless for so long that we actually forgot she was on the floor. We were watching an old black and white movie called *Quatermass and the Pit*. It was a film from the late 1950s, where a scientist called Quatermass investigates some strange artefacts found in an underground station in London. We had just got the point where he discovered an alien spacecraft that had been buried there hundreds of years ago. The lights started failing and the suspense was building when we heard it... a faint voice that said: "Has he gone?" Quatermass looked around but couldn't see anything, so he walked further into the darkness. Then the voice came again. "Has he gone?" But this time it was louder, and a little annoyed that Quatermass hadn't replied.

Quatermass said, "Is anyone there?"

There was a flash in the darkness and at the same time my mother sat up, really annoyed now, and shouted: "Has he bloody gone or not?!" She scared the shit out of us! After a few minutes of laughing and crying, Mike said he had. Mum immediately got up and walked into the kitchen, got her bowl of pasta and joined us in front of the TV, as though nothing had happened.

Now, this method of not paying your weekly loan seemed to work in the 1970s, but unfortunately, I don't think it would work these days... especially if you pay by direct debit.

Words of Wisdom: When presented with a no-win situation, pretend to be dead.

Chapter 9

Slap Me, I'm a Fat Italian Asthmatic, or The Perfect Cup of Coffee

I have had asthma all my life; I manage it with inhalers, and it doesn't really affect the quality of my life. Unfortunately, that wasn't always the case. Up until 1985, the only medication I had to control my asthma was a plastic 'dry powder inhaler'. This inhaler came with a set of capsules very much like a modern-day flu capsule, which were full of powder. You put a capsule in the inhaler, it punctured it, and you sucked on the inhaler, which made the capsule spin around and released its contents, much of which ended up stuck to the inside of your mouth. A tiny bit made its way into your lungs where, as far as I was concerned, it did bloody nothing to help me with my asthma. Consequently, if I ever had an asthma attack, I was essentially on my own. Well, I say I was on my own, but there was of course Mum. She would always be there to calm me down and rub Vicks Vapour Rub on my chest and back.

I remember always having asthma attacks in the middle of the night, when I would try to keep quiet and not disturb anyone. I would load a capsule into my inhaler, for no other reason than I was taught to do so, but I knew it wasn't going to help. I'd try to calm down and attempt to take deep breaths, but inevitably it would get to the point where I knew I had to get up. At almost the same time that I got out of bed, I would smell the scent of freshly brewed coffee wafting up the stairs. My mother would be downstairs with a fresh pot of dark coffee bubbling away on the gas cooker. When she saw me, she would say, "Vieni qui," and I would sit down while she poured me a strong cup of black coffee, loaded with sugar. I would sip the coffee and she would talk quietly to me while gently rubbing my back. I don't remember what she said; I just remember that she was always there... I don't ever remember coming downstairs and not smelling the coffee or seeing her there reading a newspaper while she waited for me. She never complained that she was losing yet another night's sleep, or at least she never complained to me. If I look back now as a son and a parent, I am both humbled and amazed by her.

Anyway, those 'middle of the night' coffee sessions usually did the trick, but occasionally not even they worked. On these occasions Mum would walk down to the conveniently located ambulance station at the end of the street. They would then send an ambulance out on what had to be their shortest callout. I would be hooked up to an oxygen supply and rushed to hospital. Generally, I would be home the next day and off school that week to recover.

There was, however, one occasion where things didn't go as planned. I remember coming downstairs as normal and sipping the coffee, but this time instead of feeling better I felt worse... much worse. In addition to the asthma attack I also started to cough, but it wasn't a normal cough. This cough was deep and loud; it resonated through my body and hurt like hell. As the asthma and cough got worse, my breathing got increasingly short. Mum was really worried this time and she ran to the ambulance station, but by the time she got back I had stopped breathing. I remember panicking and thinking I was going to die.

The ambulance driver came running in, picked me up and carried me to the ambulance. Once inside, he hooked me up to the oxygen and said: "Anthony, can you hear me? If you can, you need to calm down and breathe." I could hear him OK, but I couldn't calm down because I was bloody dying! He soon realised that things weren't looking good. Apparently, I had turned an alarming shade of blue and hadn't taken a breath in a couple of minutes. Just as I was beginning to black out, the ambulance man took the oxygen mask from my face and shook me, then shouted: "Anthony, come on, lad. Snap out of it! You know what to do!" Then he looked at my mum, then back at me. Calmly, he said: "Sorry, Anthony, but this is for your own good."

I thought, "What's for my own good... dying? What sort of medical professional are you?" But as I was thinking, he pulled back his right arm and then brought it back with such speed that I didn't realise what was happening until it landed with an almighty thwack on my left cheek. There was shock at first, then there was pain, then there was a ringing in my ears. "What the fuck was that for?" I screamed, with tears flowing down my now stinging cheek. He just smiled. "What are you smiling at, you bloody..."

Then I realised two things: the first was that I was breathing, and the second was that he knew exactly what he was doing. He could see that I had worked myself up into a frenzy and he needed to snap me out of it and give me something else to think about.

He put the oxygen mask back on me and turned to my mum, who was in tears. "He's going to be OK now," he said. "He's a bit of a tough nut, he is." He turned back to me, put his hands on my shoulders and said, "Things are rarely as bad as they seem. When this happens again, just remember what happened tonight and try to calm yourself down." He tapped me gently on my left cheek and drove me to the hospital.

Mike, Chris, Diane, me and Mum

It's funny, while writing this book I have learned so much about the origins of my personality, my quirks and my outlook on life. For example, for much of my adult life I have been in search of the perfect cup of coffee; one that smells like coffee but, crucially, one that also tastes like coffee. While writing this chapter I realised why this is so important to me. The smell of freshly brewing coffee comforts me. It reminds me that in times of trouble there was always someone downstairs waiting for me. Someone waiting to comfort me and look after me. As soon as I smelled Mum's coffee percolating on the gas cooker, I knew I was going to be OK.

I have, unknowingly, been searching for the 'perfect cup' of coffee... the coffee that is going to make everything better... my mum's coffee. But the truth is that I will never find that perfect coffee, because it only existed for the young Anthony Hyde. I have some good friends who always bring me coffee back from their travels around the world in the hope that they can help me find the elusive 'perfect cup'. I was going to tell them not to bother anymore, but then that young voice inside me said: "No... One day, when things are at their worst, you'll smell the coffee and you'll walk down those stairs again... and someone you love will be waiting for you with a cup of coffee to make things better again." So, I'm still looking...

Words of Wisdom: Never give up on your search for the perfect cup of coffee.

Chapter 10

The Magic of Food

Whatever the question, situation or mood, my mother's solution was always food. If you were sad, she would make you pasta in a rich tomato sauce with lots of cheese on top. If you were sick, then a bowl full of minestrone soup would make you better. If you were happy, pizza was the perfect partner. And if, for some unthinkable reason, you weren't hungry... she would make chips!

Although Mum had to continually figure out how she was going to feed us on an extremely limited budget, she didn't see it as an arduous and thankless task. For her, it was a way to bring the family together... it was a way to show her love. She spent the majority of her time trying to be strong and hide her worries from us, so when she smiled, you knew she was truly happy. She smiled when I sang the lead solo in the school play... she smiled at my graduation... she smiled on my wedding day... she smiled when she held my daughters... but mostly, she smiled when we were enjoying her food... and she beamed when we asked for more.

When we were young, food would also denote the day of the week. On Fridays, when Mum got paid, we would have fish 'n' chips and a large bottle of dandelion and burdock from the local chippy. On Saturdays, when she went out to do the weekly shop, we would have luxuries from the local delicatessen: crusty Italian bread, mortadella, salami, cheese, and chillies... Sunday would be a roast.

As the week went on and the food slowly ran out, we reverted to simple pasta dishes, pizza and chips. Thursdays would be the worst day for food, because there would be either nothing in the cupboards or a collection of random ingredients. This meant that Mum had to be creative with her cooking. We would have things like 'all in pie'. You can guess what's coming... She would take a large baking tray and line it with pastry made from flour and water, then collect all the ingredients she had left in the kitchen and throw them in, then top it with another layer of pastry. As you would expect, this resulted in some very unusual flavour combinations. Pickled beetroot and potatoes were often the main ingredients... and sometimes just potatoes. It was an effort to eat, not just because of the contents, but also because the pastry was so hard that you needed a hammer to break through.

Even the pie was seen as a luxury on the days when there was nothing left in the cupboards. On those days, she would resort to the classic 'coffee toffee'. She would melt sugar in a pan, add instant coffee, then pour it onto the table. When it cooled, she would break it up and we would have coffee sweets. She did the best she could... and now that I have a family of my own, I am in awe of her and what she did. When I think about it now, she could have bought food that would have lasted us to the end of the week, but it would have been basic. Instead, she made the conscious decision to buy luxuries for the first few days of the week, because she wanted us to enjoy food and look forward to it. Forty years on, and I can still remember the wonderful food we had at the weekends. She gave me a gift... a passion for food.

Not only have I inherited her passion for food, but I have also gained her selfless pleasure of cooking and feeding family and friends. I spend hours preparing and cooking food, not because I want to impress or because I want praise, but because I want to give enjoyment. It makes me so happy to think that people remember eating my food. Some people treat food purely as sustenance... and there is nothing wrong with that. They tend not to have food-related memories and will often forget what they had for dinner the previous evening. For me, food is far more than just sustenance. It is love and friendship... it is caring... it is fun and laughter. When I hear friends talking about the food I made at a party years ago, it makes me so proud.

It's worth saying here that you don't have to be a great cook to give and receive pleasure from cooking. After all, I wouldn't say Mum was a great cook, but that was never the point. She did, however, have a few signature dishes that were brilliant. Top of the list were her chips (French fries, for any Americans reading this). Even now, my mouth is salivating as I think of having one of her chip butties after coming home from a night out. I made it my life's goal to make the perfect bowl of chips. I now have a tried-and-tested method that may take a lot of effort but delivers the most wonderful triple-cooked chips. But here's the thing... My mum would just cut up any old potatoes and chuck them into the frying pan... and, ten minutes later, there would be a plate full of brilliant chips! I just don't understand it. How could she make such amazing chips without even trying? I guess that's the magic touch.

Second on her list of comfort foods was her wonderful 're-heated pasta'. Like her chips, it was legendary. When I first brought Debbie home, Mum asked her if she wanted any reheated pasta. Debbie looked at me quizzically. "What's reheated pasta?"

I said: "Do you know pasta? Well, it's that, but cooked twice." I think she threw a shoe at me. So... reheated pasta is exactly what it sounds like. You cook pasta in the normal way; you drain the pasta and add it to a pan of tomato sauce. You stir it all together, take it off the heat, put the pan lid on and leave it... the longer the better. This gives time for the sauce to be absorbed into the pasta. When you come to reheat the pasta, you put a drizzle of olive oil in and stir continually until it's nice and hot. Dish out into bowls with a fresh grating of parmigiana cheese on the top... and enjoy. It's so wonderfully luxurious and tasty... it just melts in your mouth. I know everyone goes on about 'al dente' pasta, but as far as I am concerned, the best thing to do with 'al-dente' pasta is to stick it in a pan and have it the next day. Why would you want raw pasta anyway? I know... I know... Every time there is an interview on TV with an Italian chef, they always go on about the rest of the world overcooking pasta. But I bet you, as soon as they get home, they heat up a pan of yesterday's pasta and snuggle up in front of the television with a loved one.

Finally, there was mum's mammoth fried breakfast. Like her chip butties, which were designed for the evening after a good night out, her breakfasts were designed for the morning after. Fried eggs, sausages, bacon, beans, mushrooms, plum tomatoes, lashings of toast and gallons of coffee. Debbie and I loved coming home for the weekend when we were still studying and waking up on the Saturday morning to the smell of breakfast being cooked.

Unfortunately, not all Mum's dishes were so wonderful. Her pizzas were... well... essentially, thick slices of bread with tomato sauce and cheese on top. I'm sure this type of pizza has its roots in the poverty-stricken Italy of her youth, designed to be a cheap way to fill you up, which they certainly did.

Her gnocchi was so heavy, it could have sunk a battleship. It was, however, responsible for one of the most iconic Italian memories from childhood. Once every couple of months Mum would set aside a day for making gnocchi. Every surface in the kitchen would be covered with rows and rows of little potato/pasta dumplings. We would wait impatiently all day for her to say: "It's ready!" Then there would be a stampede as we all rushed to get a bowl full of the dumpling delights. Looking back now, I think she was one of the first people to cook with Rohypnol. I say this with certainty, because after the second mouthful of these lead-weighted, stodgy dough-balls, we couldn't believe how bad they were. We couldn't believe we had forgotten how heavy they were. I was always careful not to go swimming after having some of my mum's gnocchi for fear of sinking. It wasn't until I went to Italy as an adult that I realised gnocchi was supposed to be light and fluffy.

Then there were her 'lottery meat dishes'... For example,

she would often buy the cheapest steak, with the best of intentions, only to realise that after frying, it was rather tough. This didn't deter her, oh no. After frying the steak she would then boil it to soften it up, but in doing so, she would boil all the flavour from it... but this wasn't a problem, because she just fried it again to crisp it up. By the time it was served, it was just a piece of brown meat-like substance. Luckily, when we were kids, we had a dog and we would feed him the 'lottery meat' when Mum wasn't looking. The dog could only take two or three servings before he would start to retch and vomit under the table. So you had to get in there quick, otherwise you would be the only one left with meat on your plate... and that was a big no-no. Mum would stand over you until you cleaned your plate. Unfortunately, the dog wasn't with us long... No, he didn't die; he ran away.

Unsurprisingly, at the age of sixteen, I became a vegetarian. I don't think Mum ever really understood it. When I tried to explain it to her, she nodded and said: "But you can still eat chicken though?"

I laughed and said "No! No meat... no chicken, no ham, no beef and no lamb!" On the evening I told her, she came out of the kitchen with a plate of sandwiches and inside was... yes, you guessed it... wafer thin ham. "Mummmm...! I said no meat!"

She said, "But it's wafer thin?" And before you say that was a line from the film *My Big Fat Greek Wedding*... that film was released in 2002, whereas this happened in 1983.

So, that's when I started cooking for myself. This memory is tinged with a little guilt, because it's only now as I write this page that I realise how that action of independence may also have taken away one of the things Mum enjoyed... cooking for me.

The smell, taste and look of food evoke such memories for me. I will always think of Mum when I dip a piece of buttered crusty bread into a pan of pasta sauce. The smell of percolating Italian coffee when I was ill. The smell of fish 'n' chips on a clear cold night... Whenever she won at bingo, she would stop off at the chippy on the way home and as she opened the door, the smell of chips, alcohol and fresh air was intoxicating.

To earn more money, she worked the night shift for a short time. She was paid on the Friday morning, so she would stop off on the way home and buy Blue Riband chocolate wafers, XL crisps and bottles of Coke for breakfast. Not the healthiest of breakfasts, but I still remember them with such fondness.

I suspect everyone has memories like these, or at least I hope they do, because they can be so evocative. I have taken great pleasure in generating similar sorts of memories for my kids... and their friends. I say this because we always seemed to have our children's friends around at mealtimes. They were big fans of my cooking. They have all grown up now and scattered around the country, either studying or in their first jobs. I see them rarely, but out of the blue one of Emma's friends, Reilee, phoned her up. He was excited and asked her what the herb was that I used to cook with most. Emma said it would probably have been oregano, to which he shouted, "I knew it! I smelled a fresh herb today and all I could think about was sitting in your kitchen while your dad was cooking."

That comment made me so happy, but it horrified my eldest daughter... "Do you mean to say I went to school smelling of oregano?!" Well, one man's pleasure is another woman's embarrassment...

Words of Wisdom: Make time to share good food and good wine with family and friends... and you will have memories that will keep you warm on the coldest of nights.

Chapter 11
The Ouija Board

Growing up as a Roman Catholic gives you a certain superiority complex over other religions – and other Catholics, for that matter. I had no idea what the difference was between a Roman Catholic and a Catholic. I just thought we were 'real Catholics'. I was led to believe we were part of an exclusive club that had a direct line to the Pope. And that we carried the hopes and guilt of the world... and oh boy, did we carry the guilt. The number of times I heard: "The lord gave up his son to wash away our sins. He died on the cross... for you!" Especially from Sister O'Brien, a particularly scary nun who used to turn up at the school unannounced. She would pick on a random boy and just stare into his eyes – into his very soul – with her piercing, all-knowing eyes. The unlucky boy would have to stare back and could not avoid her gaze, or he would feel her wrath. After an agonising few minutes she would whisper, "I see your sin, boy, and God sees your sin... If you don't stop your evil ways you'll go blind and if you don't repent you will burn in hell." She was by far the scariest woman I have ever known – and she starred in some of my worst childhood nightmares. She even made one boy wet himself he was so scared, which just made her angrier... until, that is, the priest walked past, at which point her craggy, evil, contorted face turned angelic as she swivelled around and said: "Oh Father, I didn't know you would be here today. What a wonderful surprise!" The boy took the opportunity to escape to the toilet to clean himself up and, instead of being cruelly teased about this event for the rest of his life, he was treated with kindness and pity, which is amazing when you consider how cruel children can be.

One thing I have learned over the years is that people who had nuns involved in their education are polarised in terms of their views on life and religion. They tend to be screwed up in some way, with most entering adult life with an irrational dislike of nuns and religion. Although we moved around quite a lot when I was young, we always went to Catholic schools and most of them had lessons that were taught by monks from the local monastery and nuns from the local nunnery.

The monks came in two versions: the first was the younger, cooler brother, who wanted you to see how great being a monk was. He would always be smiling and trying to crack jokes. He thought he was 'down with the kids', whatever that means. He would also be the one who would come out with a fable to meet every situation, but he updated his fables and they were so annoying. They would go something like this: "I'd like to tell you about something that happened to me today. I was walking down the road and I met a man with a dog. I said to the man, 'Does your dog bite?' And he said, 'No.' So I bent down to pat the dog and it bit me. I was enraged and turned to the man and shouted, 'I thought you said your dog didn't bite?' He said, 'It doesn't,' and looked at the dog that had just bitten me and said, 'That's not my dog.'"

We all giggled, and if he had left it there he would have earned some 'cool' points. Oh no, he couldn't leave it there... He went on to say: "...and that reminded me of Jesus and what he had to say about anger. He said, 'I tell you that anyone who is angry with his brother will be subject to judgement. Therefore, if you are offering your gift at the altar...'" He went on for ages, quoting from the Bible, then comparing it to the dog's nature, the man's lack of compassion and his inability to control his anger. What did I learn? Don't pat a strange dog.

The second type of monk was older and much more... monkish? They were a bit scary, a bit dark, but somehow cooler than the younger monks who spent all their time trying, unsuccessfully, to be cool. A lot of them had rather red noses and cheeks. At first I thought it was because it was always cold outside. Then someone said that they brewed their own beer and wine in the monastery.

Nuns also came in two versions. The first was the quiet ones, who rarely came into school because they were terrified of people. The second was the angry ones. What were they angry about? I've got no idea. They took their anger out on children, because they were sinners. As far as the angry nuns were concerned, all the girls were sleeping with older men and the boys were masturbating themselves blind. The only time they weren't angry was in the presence of a priest... Oh no, then they were angels.

Now I think about it, I don't have any memories of monks and nuns being at our school at the same time... and they never really talked about each other. Let's analyse this a bit more: you never saw them together, they both wore dresses, they both insisted that masturbating would make you go blind, and they both agreed that the devil was all around us and was always trying to tempt us, and that we should stay away from Ouija boards. I know what you're thinking... Was there just one set of cross-dressing individuals from a 'monnary'...? OK... I'm going to hell for that one.

When I was about eight years old, everyone was into all things scary. *The Exorcist* had just been released and everyone was talking about it. It was even on the news, where they showed clips of people coming out of cinemas looking shocked. There were interviews with concerned mothers, and forthright priests preaching about how the film was encouraging the young to experiment with Ouija boards, which wasn't so far from the truth. It seemed like everyone either had a scary story to tell about what happened to them when they used one, or they knew someone who had a scary encounter. You were seen as cool if you had a Ouija board and even cooler if you'd used it.

Step forward one of my brother's friends, who had just acquired a board. He and my brother arranged for a group of their friends to come around to our house to have a seance. I think our house was chosen because it had a small and very dark cellar. They waited until a Friday night, when they knew our mum would be out. I remember Chris was a bit anxious, because Mum was debating whether to go or not, because Mike wasn't back yet and she didn't want to leave Chris in charge. He convinced her that everything would be OK and that Mike would be home soon. She eventually agreed and left reluctantly.

As soon as she had disappeared around the corner of our street, a swarm of boys descended on our front door. One of them was carrying a sack containing the Ouija board, two black candles and a big bag of sweets. The house was filled with a heady concoction of excitement, anticipation and, of course, varying levels of fear. They were giggling and playing tricks on each other in an attempt to scare someone – and, possibly, to take their minds off the fact that they were scared. Chris said I wasn't allowed to join in. I had to be lookout, just in case Mum came back. Like a good Catholic Italian boy, I obeyed my brother's instructions... So, when they had all gone down to the basement and switched the lights off, I switched off all the downstairs lights and slowly opened the cellar door. They didn't notice me sneaking down the stairs, partly because it was very dark and partly because they were still giggling and messing about. I stopped about halfway down the stairs and settled on the cold stone step to watch.

It took them an eternity to calm down and arrange themselves around the Ouija board, but once they did, everything became deadly quiet. It was the sort of silence that I can only describe as heavy. It was very dark, very quiet and *very* scary. Of course, with a bunch of teenage boys this didn't last long, and the mood was lightened by my brother Chris... who farted.

There were yells and screams. "You dirty bastard!" shouted one boy.

"Oh my God, I'm gonna die... it stinks!" shouted

another.

"Quick, open the cellar door!" shouted a third.

Of course, I was gasping too, and was just about to go back up the stairs to open the door when I remembered that I wasn't supposed to be there. I heard footsteps and started to panic as someone approached me on the stairs. But, to my relief, it was soon followed by another voice that said: "No, don't open the door, because you'll let the light in, and it'll spoil the mood." The footsteps departed and I sighed with relief.

They settled down again, but this time there was a blinding flash as a match was ignited on the cellar floor and the boy who had brought the Ouija board, Jimmy, lit a solitary candle and placed it on a ledge on the wall. It cast enough light that they could read the letters on the board, but not enough to spoil the atmosphere – and, more crucially, not enough to penetrate the darkness that was hiding me. Once my eyes became accustomed to the new light level, I could clearly see the boys huddled around the Ouija board and I could just make out some lettering and markings on it, but I couldn't read anything. While they were arranging themselves I looked around the cellar; I had never had the guts to go down there before. I could just about see the far end of the cellar because there was a mirror resting against the wall and it reflected the glow from the candle. Mostly the rest of the cellar was in darkness, with only the odd shape here and there.

"Right, everyone put a finger on the blanket," Jimmy said. It wasn't until years later that I learned what he meant to say was 'planchette'. Anyway, back to the cellar. Jimmy carried on. "Is anyone there?" Silence... "Is anyone there...? If you can hear me, then give us a sign." The planchette started to move...

"That was you, Dave!" said one boy.

"No, it wasn't!" Dave said, trying to stifle a giggle.

"Right, c'mon... stop pissing about," said Jimmy. He started again. "Is anyone there? If you can hear me then give us a sign." This time there was no movement of the planchette so Jimmy tried again. "If there is a spirit present, could you let us know you are here?"

This time, something caught my eye in the corner of the cellar. Against the glow in the mirror I could just about make out the outline of... a person. A cold shiver engulfed me... I was petrified. I looked at the boys around the Ouija board. One, two, three, four, five... they were all there... I looked back to the mirror. Since I had just been looking at the candle everything was black again, so I had to wait. As I focused back on the darkness, I could make out the shadow again. There was definitely something there... or was it there before and I just didn't notice it? No... I definitely remember seeing the glow of the candlelight in the mirror and there was nothing masking it. There was definitely the shape of a shoulder and a head. As I looked closer and concentrated really hard, it moved! I froze.

Now, everything that happened next must have taken seconds, but in my mind it lasted minutes. One of the boys must have seen something move in the shadows, because I heard him shout, "What the fuck, what the fuck, fuck fuck!" He pointed to the darkness as he stood up and ran up the stairs. Then all hell broke loose as the rest of the boys began to scream and shout and stampede towards the stairs and the cellar door. I was still in shock and hadn't moved. The first boy was scrambling up the stairs on his hands and feet, and when he got to me his hand landed on my face and I screamed. Well... he screeched and flew backwards down the stairs, taking the other boys with him!

Sometime during this frenzy, I bolted through the cellar door and didn't stop running until I was outside the house on the cobbles on the opposite side of the street. My heart was pounding, and I was sweating so much that I soon started to shiver in the cool night air. I was staring back at our front door when five terrified teenagers came racing out. They scattered in all directions, and all but one came to a stop at a safe distance from the house to look back and shout... well... shout lots more phrases of wonderment and surprise at what had just happened. One boy didn't stop to turn around and just kept on running all the way home. I found out later that he was the one who had put his hand on my face. He swore to the others that a demon had pushed him back down the stairs as he tried to escape. He was also the one who had seen the figure in the corner of the cellar. So he had a double whammy – I can totally understand why he was so terrified. I never told Chris what I had seen, and he never really talked to me about it, because as far as he was concerned, I was outside keeping watch.

A few weeks later, I remember I was in church practising with the rest of the choir for an upcoming recital. The practice had gone well, and we were chatting with the priest, as we normally did. He was one of the cool priests so a few of us always stayed late to chat with him, because he always had interesting and sometimes funny stories to tell. On this occasion he wasn't so chatty, so I asked him if everything was OK.

"Oh, I am sorry, boys," he said. "I am just a little distracted... I had a very disturbing weekend." Well, that captured our attention, and we were all wondering how we could get him tell us what happened without us sounding insensitive and rude. We needn't have worried because he went on to say, "Normally I wouldn't tell you boys things like this, but with all this interest in Ouija boards at the moment, I think it is my duty to warn you of the dangers." This was juicy, we all thought at once, and we sat down on the church pews ready for the story. "This Saturday evening, I was just closing up and getting ready to turn in for the night when there was a loud banging on the front door of the vicarage. I rarely get visitors late in the evening, so I rushed to answer it. I was greeted by three teenagers: two boys and a girl. The two boys were sweating and out of breath and they were carrying the girl, who seemed to be unconscious. The boys were terrified and were pleading with me to let them in. Naturally, I beckoned them in while asking them what had happened. The boys were frantically recounting something, but I couldn't understand them because they were talking at the same time... and to be honest they were talking gibberish. After they laid the girl on the couch, I asked them to calm down and start again, but this time I asked only one of them to tell me what had happened."

The priest leaned against the pulpit and went on. "The boy I asked took a deep breath and said they had been in the disused cotton mill. He said they were just messing about, just having a bit of fun... and they didn't mean any harm. At this point I interrupted him and asked him what was it that they had done. He told me they had gone there with a Ouija board to have a seance. As you can imagine, I was shocked at this revelation and I couldn't hide my displeasure, but I pressed him further. I asked him what had happened to the girl. He composed himself again and said they had started the seance in the normal way, but that things started to get weird. They heard noises and then voices... The boys exchanged terrified looks and the older boy carried on. He said they were not making this up or imagining it, but the next thing that happened was so unbelievable that even now they were scared. He said objects started to fly around the building. At first it was rags and paper, so they thought it was the wind. But then boxes and wood started to fly past their heads! They knew they had to get out of the mill, so they all turned and ran to the nearest door. As they did, a brick hit the girl and she fell to the ground. So they picked her up and carried her straight to somewhere they thought they would be safe, which is why they came to me."

We looked at each other with wide eyes, like this was the best scary story we had ever heard... and it was real... well, probably... priests don't lie. "What happened then?" I asked.

The priest's face paled. "I didn't know what to think of the story. I couldn't quite believe what they said happened, but I also totally believed that something horrible had happened and they were terrified. So I told them to sit down and relax; they were safe now. I said I would make them some drinks and get a first aid kit for the girl, but first I would phone for an ambulance."

He paused, then said, "I went into the hallway and called for an ambulance, then on to the kitchen to make a pot of tea. I must admit, I was disturbed by the events of that evening and was distracted, so I don't remember how long I was in the kitchen. But when I came back into the front room the girl was still unconscious on the sofa, but the boys had gone. I sat with the girl until the ambulance came, then went to bed. The next morning, I was visited by two police officers who had come to take my statement. I went through the story in the same way I have just done with you boys and finished it by asking them how the girl was and had they talked to the boys. The two officers looked at each other and one officer asked me, 'Haven't you been told? The two boys were found in the early hours of the morning about a mile from here in a field.' I was confused and asked what they were doing in a field and the officer said, "I'm sorry, Father. They're both... dead.'"

You could have cut the silence with a knife. We were stunned... That was just the coolest story I'd ever been told. The priest then said he had to go and prepare for his next sermon, and he left. We were all quiet until we had left the church; then there was a cacophony of shouting and screaming. "Oh my God... that was amazing!" said one boy.

"That had to be bullshit!" shouted another.

"Why would he make it up?" said another.

We came to the collective conclusion that it had to be made up, but I guarantee you that, once we parted company to go home, each of us, deep down, believed it was real.

Words of Wisdom: If you put a sign up next to a red button that says: "Do not push this red button," you can be pretty sure someone is going to push the red button.

Chapter 12

The Ice Cream Wars and Free Ice Cream

The Manchester of my childhood was a series of long criss-crossing cobbled streets stretching into the distance. When I came out of my front door I could see a woodyard directly opposite... ah, the woodyard... well, you know all about that. If I looked to my right, I could see the ambulance station, and my primary school behind it. If I looked to my left, I could see a long street that went on and on into the distance. This view was dominated by a huge gas yard, which was one block down from the woodyard. No, it wasn't a place where people went to eat baked beans. It was where they stored natural gas for the local area. Inside the gas yard were two HUGE gas storage tanks... I think they were called gasometers. Anyway, when I say huge, I mean huge. I looked it up; they were seventy metres in diameter and sixty-five metres high. They would mysteriously move up and down as the gas in them was slowly depleted or filled. The reason I say mysteriously is because in all the time I lived on that street, I never saw them move. It was like a classic comedy sketch... I would be looking at the tanks for ages, waiting to catch them move. Then someone would call me, I would look around and talk to them, and when I looked back one of them had moved! When I was younger, I thought it was a secret government base, where they were experimenting on aliens... OK, so I had (still have!) a rather fertile imagination.

Opposite the gas yard and further on from it on the same side were terraced houses as far as the eye could see. The streets weren't lined with cars like they are now; they were lined with kids of all ages playing all kinds of games. It was like one big school playground, with all the noise that came with it. Today, most kids are inside playing computer games, which is not a bad thing. I too am a great fan of computer games. It's just that in those days we didn't have much choice but to be outside.

You would see kids playing games like marbles, kerby, British bulldog, hopscotch, skipping, hide and seek... I could go on and on. Although sometimes the noise could be deafening, there was always one child in the middle of the mayhem who would stop and look distracted. Then their head would turn, and their face would scrunch up with concentration. Then their face would relax, and the beginnings of a smile would appear, just before their eyes closed, their mouth opened and the noise everyone was waiting for came screeching out... "Ice cream vaaaaaan!"

Everyone would freeze and listen carefully... and, sure enough, we'd hear the dulcet tones of *Greensleeves* tinkling in the distance. Then, en masse, there would be a riot of screams. Kids would drop whatever they had in their hands and shoot off in every direction, all running home to persuade their parents to give them money for an ice cream. Within the space of about sixty seconds, the once busy streets would be empty... well, almost empty. The really poor kids were left behind because they knew there was no point running home to ask for money... It wasn't all bad; we had the streets to ourselves, even if it was only for a few minutes.

The ice cream van would come around the corner, blasting out its familiar melody, and park up. Just before it stopped, it would be surrounded by a mob of kids brandishing coins in the air and screaming their particular choice of ice cream. A Mr Whippy was by far the most popular – so soft and luxurious, with raspberry syrup or sprinkles on top. Every now and then, when my mum had won at bingo or had just received a new loan, she would let us have one. I would do my best to make it last as long as possible. If I had a chocolate flake with it, I would push it down though the ice cream into the cone. Then I'd break off the bottom of the cone, which was now full of ice cream, and scoop off some more ice cream from the top... and now I had two ice creams! Life is all about little pleasures. I remember doing the same for my children when they were young.

There was a time when ice cream was plentiful in the Hyde household, and that was when a new ice cream van started appearing on our street. It was driven by a man with an incredibly large nose. I do remember his name, but don't want to get into trouble, so let's say it was Johnny Lavetti. His name was in big lettering on the side of the van... Lavetti's. After a few days, I remember him turning up at our house to see my mum while we were out playing. He would visit Mum most days that summer; she said he was her 'special friend'. I didn't think anything of it, especially because of what happened the day after his first visit: he pulled up in his ice cream van as usual, but this time he called me over and gave me a free Mr Softy... which was the same as a Mr Whippy. Well, I was in seventh heaven... It was summer, the weather was beautiful, and I was getting free ice cream every day!

Mr Lavetti's van used to turn up on our street approximately thirty to forty minutes before the regular ice cream van, which was called... er... let's say Calluchi's. The man in the Calluchi van couldn't figure out why he wasn't getting the usual rush of kids. He even resorted to playing the music again while he parked up, to no avail. This went on for weeks; Mr Lavetti would turn up, I would get my ice cream, and by the time I had finished it, Calluchi's van turned up. As time went on, the man in the Calluchi's van became more and more bewildered and frustrated. Until, that is, he turned up earlier than usual one day to find us kids finishing our ice creams. Well, you could see the rage in his face. He called me over and said: "Hey kid, where did you get that ice cream from?" I told him, but as soon as he heard the name Lavetti his face went red, he closed the sliding window on his van and drove off.

The next day was one of those days that was written into local folklore. It was the sort of day worthy of inclusion in a book. It began just like any other day that summer: kids playing in the streets, Mr Lavetti's van turning up, kids getting their ice creams. However, today was a little different. Instead of Mr Calluchi's van turning up thirty to forty minutes after Mr Lavetti's had left, he turned up while Mr Lavetti was still there. To us kids, we thought it was Christmas – two ice cream vans at the same time! Unfortunately, the men driving the vans were no longer interested in us...

Mr Calluchi drove his van right up to the back of Mr Lavetti's. He jumped out and, in a flash, he was inside Mr Lavetti's van and had his hands around Mr Lavetti's throat! "What the fuck are you doing on my patch?" he shouted.

Mr Lavetti said, "Urrrgggghhh!" Well, you would, wouldn't you? Then he broke the stranglehold and they both started wrestling inside the van, pushing one way, then the other. The van was rocking from side to side and there were chocolate flakes and wafers flying everywhere. Every now and again they would press up against the ice cream machine and there would be a burst of ice cream with no cone to catch it... What a waste. The fight lasted for quite some time... I say fight, but I don't recall anyone punching anyone; they just wrestled. After ten minutes or so, they had attracted quite a crowd of people of all ages. I guess there wasn't too much on TV for adults either. The inside of Mr Lavetti's van was a mess and the two men were covered in ice cream and toppings.

Suddenly the fight burst onto the streets, where the watching crowd obligingly shifted to accommodate the spectacle. It was at this point that my 'Spidey sense' started tingling. The crowd behind me went quiet and I turned to see my mum pushing her way through. Actually, she didn't have to push anyone, because they just parted... Everyone either respected my mum or was scared of her. She got to the centre of the fight and went straight in. With her left hand she grabbed one of Mr Calluchi's ears and with her right hand she grabbed one of Mr Lavetti's ears. Then she shouted: "Stupido!" I don't think that needs translating. She separated them and slapped them both across the face... and I don't need to tell you how much that would have hurt. She then gave them an unintelligible lecture, which they listened to obediently, just like two naughty school children. Then she turned to the watching crowd and told them to bugger off, which they promptly did.

The two men wiped themselves down and drove off. It was the last time I saw Mr Lavetti – and it was the end of my free ice cream summer.

Words of Wisdom: Enjoy the free ice cream while it lasts, because it won't always be there.

Chapter 13
What, No Garlic?

I'm going to risk having my Italian member's card revoked by saying this: I hate garlic! I feel like I'm in an Alcoholics Anonymous meeting... "I am a second-generation Italian and I hate garlic." It's funny, I get no sympathy or consideration from my family and friends for this affliction. I get no sympathy when we go out to restaurants. The things I do get are: "Well, it's only a little bit of garlic," or "I think you're being over sensitive."

Oh, but it's oh so different when someone doesn't like fish or mayonnaise or Himalayan goat herder's cheese; suddenly everyone is sympathetic and will go out of their way to find alternatives. I'm not bitter... much. I hate garlic: I hate the smell, I hate the taste and, most of all, I hate smelling of garlic. The thought of breathing stale garlic onto someone fills me with dread.

It's like when I go to the gym and I am on one of those stepping machines and a bloke steps up onto the machine next to me. He sets up the machine and he's off. Then he starts to sweat... No, that's not the issue. Sweating is fine... It's the putrid smell of stale garlic that comes with it that I don't like. I feel like turning around and saying: "What did you do... shower in garlic juice?!" Well, I would if I wasn't gagging, so all I can do is get as far away from him as possible. I'm surprised anyone eats garlic anyway; I read an article about how it gives you brain damage. Fact. What... you don't remember reading it? I rest my case.

The rant doesn't finish there. I have switched between being vegetarian and pescatarian most of my adult life. Why? Because I want to, and because I can. So, ideally, when I go out to eat in restaurants I would like to choose from the vegetarian menu, but I end up having to choose from the fish options. Why, I hear you ask? Well, it's because of the well-known fact that all vegetarians *must* have garlic in every meal... *of course they do*. So it's almost impossible for me to find anything to eat when I go out.

"What are you talking about?" I hear you say. Well, let's look at the facts. If you go to a restaurant for breakfast and order a sausage, you will usually get a pork sausage seasoned with salt and pepper and *no garlic*. The vegetarian alternative will invariably have garlic in it... *of course it does*. I love pies; when I ate meat, I would love a good steak or chicken pie and they had *no garlic* in them, but just about 90% of vegetarian alternatives *have* garlic in them... *of course they do*. One of the most ridiculous occasions was when I went to a vegetarian takeaway that advertised a fish finger sandwich. I thought, "Brilliant... I'll have one of those." So I went to the counter and was just about to order one when the little voice in my head said: "You'd better check." So I said, "Could you tell me whether the fish finger sandwich has any garlic in it?" The person serving gave me the 'Is there garlic in this?' look, which is a combination of disbelief and 'Who gives a shit?'. He went to the back of the kitchen and had a chat with the manager, who looked at me and also gave me the 'Is there garlic in this?' look.

After an intense discussion, he came back and said: "Yes, it does have garlic." *Of course it does!* Why would you put garlic in a fish finger alternative...? Why?!

I love cooking, so I just don't understand why chefs resort to garlic every time they want to impart flavour into vegetarian and vegan dishes. I am essentially a pescatarian and my two daughters are vegan, so I have spent years creating non-meat dishes that are packed with flavour, and I have never once thought, "This dish could be improved with a big lump of garlic." I just think it's a lazy option.

My wife said: "Instead of moaning about it, why don't you write a cook book and show people?" So, after I have finished writing this book, I am going to write a cook book and it will be for everyone – meat eaters, pescatarians, vegetarians and vegans – and there will be no garlic in any of the recipes, just flavour.

Rant over. So now for the analysis. Why do I hate garlic? My mum didn't cook with garlic, but she used to eat it for its health benefits. Whenever she felt ill or under the weather, she would grab a bulb of garlic and bite into it as though it was an apple. She once twisted her ankle and decided to rub garlic into it... My mother's obsession with the health benefits of garlic would be enough reason to scar me for life and instigate my hatred of garlic. But I think there was one particular event that sealed my hatred... It happened when I was around twelve years old.

There was a family Christmas get together at my Auntie

Pina's house. She had laid on a feast, with turkey, ham, roast potatoes and all the trimmings. She must have had a few kilogrammes of garlic that she wanted to use up, because the turkey and the ham were infused with garlic... No, that's being kind... the turkey and pig were drowned in a vat of garlic before they were butchered. And when she received them, she thought there just wasn't enough garlic in them, so she added four or five whole bulbs. Then there were the potatoes... She thought, "We have garlic turkey and we have garlic ham, but what we need is some more garlic," so she decided to add one clove of garlic for every potato. I also think there was garlic gravy, but there was no way anyone could have tasted it with all the garlic everywhere else on the plate. When we turned up on her doorstep and the door opened, you can understand why my nostrils instantly closed shut and I started to gag. After some oxygen and antibiotics, I managed to acclimatise myself and sat down at the dining table.

The item that is at the centre of my life-long repetitive nightmare is a ham joint. This particular ham joint had a two-centimetre-thick layer of fat around it and was swimming in garlic. I think it was doing the back stroke. A member of the party, who shall remain nameless, was the first to attack the ham. She cut a thick slice for herself, then added turkey and a good helping of the rest of the dishes on offer. Although I didn't hate garlic at the time, I do remember finding it very difficult to eat anything, because I just didn't like the taste that much.

While I was moving food around my plate, something caught my attention out of the corner of my eye. It was the nameless family member, who was cutting the thick layer of fat away from her ham steak. I, like everyone else, thought she was cutting the fat away so she could eat the ham unhindered. Unfortunately, we were all totally wrong. Once she had freed the fat layer from the ham, she picked it up with her fingertips and raised it up above her head. This attracted everyone's attention. The fifteen-centimetre length of garlic-infused white fat was just hanging there, dripping fat onto her lap. "My favourite bit!" she said. She put the free end of the ham fat in her mouth and proceeded to suck the rest in, bit by bit. With every slurping suck, there was a dribble of garlic fat down her face. It was the most repulsive thing I think I have ever seen.

After that, I lost my appetite; I said I was sick and went to the toilet. I must have been in there a long time, because the next thing I remember was coming downstairs to see some people were leaving. One of them was the 'nameless' one. She was giving everyone a Christmas kiss goodbye. I suddenly found myself in the queue and I started to panic, and with good cause. As she got to the person next to me, I could still see the fat glistening on her lips and chin. She turned to me. "Come here, darling, and give us a kiss." She put her hands either side of my face and pulled me in for the kiss. All I remember was a pair of garlic lips coming to devour me. I had been holding my breath for the last sixty seconds, so by the time she got to me I was gasping for air. I had no choice... I had to breath. I took a huge life-saving breath – along with a life-ending wave of garlic aroma... I think I blacked out.

And ever since that day I have hated garlic.

Words of Wisdom: Garlic is the devil's bum juice and the domain of the unimaginative cook.

Chapter 14

An Englishman's Home is His Castle, but an Italian's Castle is His Family

I remember re-enacting Monty Python sketches as a kid, everything from the *Dead Parrot* to the *Nudge Nudge* sketch. But the one I remember doing the most was *The Four Yorkshiremen*. Partly because it was funny, and partly because it was about people from 'up north', and we could do the accents. I should really have started this chapter with the line: "Well, of course we had it tough..." because for me and my family it was the truth. We were very poor, although I'm not sure I realised how poor we were at the time. I knew we didn't have the things that other people had, like high street clothes, the latest trainers, new bikes and cool games, but I don't remember dwelling on it. I don't ever remember being jealous or envious. Sure, I wanted things, but I never wanted other people's things and I certainly didn't resent them for having cool stuff.

If I saw someone with a cool bike, I wouldn't sit and brood about how life was unfair and how I deserved a bike just as much as they did. What I actually did was think of ways that I could get a bike. I knew I wasn't that good at making money, so that wasn't an option, but I was good at making things. So, I went off to the local scrap yard and rubbish tip and hunted around for bike parts. I'd find a frame from one place, handlebars from another, one wheel here and one there. Over a period of a few weeks I had collected enough parts to make a complete bike. I had no idea how to make a bike – and, unfortunately, I didn't have YouTube to help me. But I knew what a bike looked like and I had the bits and some tools, so I jumped in head first. I spent the next few weeks slowly putting all the bits together, until I had what resembled a bike. I was so chuffed and proud. I couldn't wait to take it out for a ride, but I resisted, because it needed cleaning up and painting.

I managed to find a handful of tiny paint tins that my eldest brother Mike used for painting his small model planes. They would only cover a small area, but they would do. So, I set about hand-painting the frame a shiny gloss black, which took me hours. When I had finished the frame, I turned my attention to the wheels, which were all tarnished and dirty. I polished them until you could see your face in them... well, not your face... I mean my face. The last touch was to put some olive oil on all the moving parts, and it was ready. After all, what else would a second-generation Italian use?

I remember when I took my bike on its first test ride. It was a dark, cold night; it had been raining earlier so the ground was wet, but the sky was crystal clear. I pushed the bike quietly out of the back door.

"Where are you going?" said Mum from the living room. I swear that woman had the whole house rigged with cameras and motion sensors.

"Nowhere," I said, and that seemed to appease her. I

came around to the front of the house and wheeled the bike onto the road, listening for the unmistakable 'click... click... click' as the bike free-wheeled into position.

I switched on the lights, which I had found at the tip that very morning, mounted the bike and... I was off! There was no one around, so I had the streets to myself and it was amazing... I had a bike! It gleamed in the lamplight as I rode down the street. I could see flashes of light reflecting from the new paintwork of the frame, from the shiny chrome of the wheel rims and from the puddles on the road. It was hypnotic and exhilarating. That night I wasn't poor, and I wasn't a fat greasy wop... I was just a normal kid with a bike. That's not quite true, because I wasn't normal... I had built my own bike and it was better than anyone else's! Well, in my little world it was. That memory and that feeling has stayed with me and I know it has shaped me. I never took that bike for granted. I appreciated how fortunate I was to have it and I looked after it... and that's how I treat most things in my life.

I built quite a few bikes over the years and each time the bike would be slightly bigger and more elaborate. I never dreamed about owning a new bike, like most of my friends. I was just content to have my hand-made one. I do, however, remember the first time I did get a brand-new bike; it was just before my seventeenth birthday.

Earlier that year my brother Chris had had an accident at work and lost half a finger. He worked at an engineering factory, making nuts and bolts. He was working on the lathe, as he normally did, when he was distracted by a friend who shouted a question at him. When he turned around to reset the lathe, he noticed there was blood everywhere. He looked at his hand and then at his finger – or, more precisely, where his finger should have been. Instead of a complete index finger there was just a stump, and from the end was a fountain of blood pouring over the lathe. He hadn't felt a thing, but at that point the pain came flooding in and he felt faint. His boss rushed him to hospital, which was about twenty minutes away. All the way there Chris kept mumbling: "I've lost my finger... I've lost my finger."

When they arrived in the emergency department of the hospital, Chris explained what had happened to the doctor, who removed the cloth from around his hand and said: "Where is the severed finger?" Chris and his boss looked at each other... they even checked their pockets, but no finger. I kid you not, they checked their pockets. Anyway, Chris's boss got back in the car and sped back to the factory to look for the finger. He eventually found it at the bottom of the lathe's sump, where all the waste collected. He had to rummage in the sludge for some time before he found it. He washed it, wrapped it up and put it on a box of frozen fish fingers... The doctor told him to put it on a bag of frozen peas, but fish fingers would have to do.

Finger secured, he jumped into his car and sped off back to the hospital. When he arrived, he presented the package to the doctor with great pride. As the doctor unwrapped it, Chris's boss regaled the story of how he found it and he was mid-stream when the doctor pulled out the mangled, metal-shaving-encrusted, dirty, smelly finger. The doctor looked at the finger and then at Chris. "Bang goes your career as a concert pianist, Chris," he said.

Roll on a few months and Chris was awarded a large amount of money in compensation... and one of the first things he did was to buy me a wonderful 'new' red racing bike. It gives me a warm feeling just thinking about it, especially as he is no longer with us. My wonderful brother died in 2019 at the age of fifty-seven and I miss him dearly. I remember writing an announcement on Facebook – it was the sort of thing I would never have done before, but I was so distraught that I was compelled to scream about his loss to the world... and I do so again today, and for as long as this book is read. This is what I wrote:

"Today the world needs to know it has lost one of its most beautiful souls in Christopher Hyde. My heart aches like no other ache before. The brightest light it has been my privilege to know has dimmed... It hasn't been extinguished, because a little piece lives on in the lives of everyone he touched. My brother is gone but will never ever be forgotten."

Chris was what I strive to be. He was selfless and loving, generous and kind... and he was the epicentre of a loving family. And that family was the most important thing in his life. I know you're thinking, "Wow... where did that come from?" The truth is that this book is just writing itself. As I sit here at the keyboard it's flowing out of me and I have no control about what comes out and the truth is... I don't want to control it. I can always move things around later, but for now I just want to write all this stuff down. This will be a record of his existence... a record that can be corroborated by anyone who knew him... and when they have all gone, this will stand as proof that such a wonderful man existed.

Self-indulgent eulogy over. As I said, I don't ever remember feeling jealous or envious of someone who had more than me. If anything, it spurred me on and gave me dreams to aspire to. I would dream of going to university and meeting the girl of my dreams. I dreamed that I would marry and have children and give them the things I never had. I would teach them to be grateful for what they had and not to envy others. I also dreamed that I would become an astronaut, and develop the ability to move objects with the power of my mind...

Now, a significant number of my dreams ended up coming true, but I had to work at it. I didn't want what other people had; I didn't want to be better than them. I just wanted to be the best version of me I could. I guess at the end of the day, I just wanted to be happy – and family was the central part of that. Family is the thing that keeps me grounded; it's a sheltered port in a stormy sea, it's my anchor... my sanctuary. If things aren't going so well in the outside world, all I need to do is come home and raise the drawbridge and I am safe. I can relax and revive myself, ready to lower the drawbridge the following day and take on all comers.

I was going to say that with family at your core, you have the confidence to take on anything, but I stopped myself just in time. Because that is one of my all-time pet peeves – when people say: "You can do anything when you put your mind to it." No, you can't! You can't squeeze your body through the eye of a needle (and that's a real body and a real needle and you're still alive afterwards). You can't get a job as a brain surgeon without doing any training (without being arrested after your first operation), and you can't become a president or prime minister if you're stupid... OK, that's a bad example. My point is, telling people they can do anything if they wish it is just irresponsible. What I'm happy to hear is: "You can do incredible things if you put your mind to it." Oh, and while I'm on a roll... "Money can't buy you happiness." Give me a million pounds and I'll show you happy! 'Money can't buy you happiness' was made up by poor people and fridge magnet makers. I was poor and I can tell you without a shadow of a doubt I would have been much happier with lots of money. And those people who win the lottery and later that year say, "I wish I had never won the lottery, it has only brought me misery..." All I can say is: "Give me the money and I'll show you happy!"

OK, rant over... Well, actually that does remind me of a rant I had when I was on my first ever business trip. I was visiting an important client with my boss and two other colleagues. We were travelling by car from the Midlands to the North of England. Towards the end of our journey we passed through a run-down housing estate. It was obviously a very poor area. There was rubbish everywhere: old mattresses in front gardens, litter in the streets, cardboard covering cracked windows, scruffy kids playing in the street, etc.

My boss, who was an Oxford university graduate, said: "It's such a shame that people have to live in these conditions in this day and age... Poor kids."

Anger instantly swelled up inside me and flowed so quickly it bypassed my internal filter, which I must admit is quite weak at the best of times, and I shouted out loud:

"Bollocks!" The car stopped and everyone looked at me as if to say, 'What the hell was that?' I had to qualify my outburst. So I began. "I came from a far poorer area and it never looked like this. Why don't you take a closer look at those poor scruffy kids?" I pointed at the nearest group. "Take a look at the ghetto blaster at their feet, and the expensive Nike trainers. Look at him with the Sony Walkman. We could never afford anything like that – we couldn't even afford an Action Man! And as for the latest trainers... well, we used to buy second-hand trainers from the market. So, no... I don't feel sorry for them, because they have far more than I ever had.

"As for the state of the streets and gardens... well, that disgusts me. Just because you are poor, it doesn't mean you can't keep things tidy... Just because you're poor doesn't mean you can't have self-respect. My mother would be utterly mortified if the front of her house wasn't clean. We didn't have a garden, but she used to polish her front step, and wash the windows, front door and pavement outside our home. You could have eaten your breakfast off the floor it was so clean... when we had enough money for breakfast, that is. It was one of the poorest areas of Manchester, but I guarantee you that our street was one of the cleanest... so... no... I have no sympathy."

There was silence again, but this time it wasn't shock and disbelief, it was perhaps an understanding... or maybe they just thought I was a nutter. No one knew what to say, because it was so alien to them, and I guess they didn't want to say anything for fear of sounding ignorant and insensitive.

As we drove off again, I had time to reflect. "Where on

earth did that outburst come from?" I thought. It had struck a raw nerve, but why? Then I started to think about it, and I realised I was angered more by the thought of those people not trying to make the best of what they had. Their home was supposed to be a haven, but they just treated it like a rubbish dump. They expected someone else to clear it up.

The people I was looking at weren't starving. They had money for clothing. They just appeared to have no respect for their community or themselves. As I write this I know how inflammatory it is, but I am just describing how I felt at the time... and remember, this wasn't an old man harping on about the good old days, this was a young man who couldn't quite understand what he was seeing and feeling.

The twenty-year-old me was thinking that the type of community he grew up in was diminishing... and to a certain extent he believed that was a good thing, because then there would be fewer people struggling to feed their families, fewer people living in rat- and cockroach-infested houses. But he was also thinking that it was a bad thing, because the values and principles of those communities seemed to be fading with them.

Now I know I am painting a swathe of people with the same brush and they may be aggrieved and affronted if they read this book; they may even take to social media to condemn me. But when I think about it, the sort of people I am talking about here are not the sort of people who will want to read this book. The sort of person who is going to read this book has compassion and principles, let's be truthful. The sort of person who is going to read this book is either a family member or a friend, plus the odd person who bought it because they thought it was about the pop group ABBA. The intention behind my writing has always been to tell family and friends about me and my life, warts and all... Can I just be clear, I do not have warts.

Words of Wisdom: You don't need money to have love and self-respect. You can do incredible things if you put your mind to it – and money can make you happy.

Chapter 15

From Hairy Jumpers to Racing Pigeon Pie

When I look back at all the stories I have about Mum, there are so many that just don't lend themselves to having a chapter on their own. So I decided that, rather than omit them, I would put them all together. These are generally the stories I love to tell people, or they just make me chuckle. I'm not telling them to poke fun or offend... but to finish the jigsaw puzzle that is Margherita Hyde.

My hairy jumper

I came home one weekend wearing a mohair jumper, which was a present from my now mother-in-law. It was jet black, with hundreds of tiny white flecks in the weave... and I loved it.

Mum took one look at it and said: "What have you been doing? Giva to me and I wash."

I wasn't quite sure what she was going on about, but then it clicked, so I said: "It's not dirty... it's supposed to be like this."

She immediately put her hand up and said, "Please yourself." It was late, and I had learned to take what Mum said with a pinch of salt, so I just shrugged my shoulders and smiled. We had some supper, chatted and went to bed.

I didn't think any more about it until the next day, when I went to put on my new jumper, but I couldn't find it. After five or ten head-scratching minutes I gave up and went downstairs for breakfast. Mum was there to greet us and pointed towards the table, which had been laid with one of her wonderful English breakfasts. As I sat down, I said: "Mum, have you seen my new jumper?"

She smiled and, with pride, went into the kitchen and returned with a black jumper. It *looked* like my jumper, but it didn't have the white mohair flecks that I loved. "I washed it and stayed up all night pulling out the cat hairs... it took me hours," she said.

I started to say: "What cat hairs..." then Debbie elbowed me in the ribs. Reluctantly, I continued: "Oh... the cat hairs... that's great... thank you." What else could I do? Well, I didn't really like the white flecks in my jumper anyway...

Haircuts 1

As a kid, I don't think I ever went to a barber's. Mainly because we couldn't afford it, but also because Mum couldn't understand why anyone would want to pay someone else to cut your hair when you could cut it yourself, for free. She had no real sense of self-image and consequently couldn't understand why her children might be concerned about having a 'hairstyle'. It's not that we wanted a hairstyle, it was more like we didn't want to look stupid... and boy, did we look stupid after one of my mum's haircuts! She never had a bowl big enough, so we always ended up with a monk's cut. The fringe would be about two centimetres above our eyebrows and that hairline would carry on all around the head... only to be punctuated – and I mean *punctuated* – by our mangled ears. They would invariably have gouges cut out of them and dribbles of blood. Mum would say: "Well, stop moving and I won't cut your ears!" So, you can imagine one of our most hated phrases from childhood was: "Time for a haircut."

It would go a little like this... I would come home from school and walk into the front room. The furniture in the front room would have been pushed against the walls and terror would engulf me... There would be a blanket on the floor, and on the blanket would be a chair... the *chair of death*. Mum would be standing next to the chair with a huge pair of scissors.

My immediate response would be to start crying and say something like: "No...! No...! I don't need a haircut!" Mum would be unmoved and just point to the chair. The next stage would be to plead. "Please Mum... Please... I'm good... Honest, we can do it next week... I promise." Still unmoved, she would just point to the chair again.

I knew there was no point in resisting so I would reluctantly sit down, and she would put a sheet under my chin and tie it behind my neck. Of course, it would be far too tight, and I would pretend that it was choking me, but she had learned to ignore me. She would then bend down to pick up the *bowl of shame* and place it on my head... Yes, people really did use bowls. When someone says they had a *basin haircut*, it means they had a large pudding bowl or mixing bowl on their head to guide the scissors during a haircut. I have since learned that it is also called a *mushroom cut* or *bowl cut* around the world. But whatever it's called, it is hideous and cruel.

The day after 'haircut day', I would dread going into school. I knew I would be ridiculed by children and teachers alike. Apparently, it builds character... Have you noticed that most dictators and mass murderers have basin haircuts?

Racing pigeons

Racing pigeons were quite a big thing in the north of England when I was growing up. Many middle-aged men kept pigeons in their backyards and raced them at weekends. These birds would often get better attention than the men's wives. We had one such man who lived in the street behind us and his backyard was fairly close to ours. It was close enough for us to hear and smell the pigeons. Mum hated them; she thought they were dirty and attracted rats. They also used to keep her up at night. She did complain, many times, but the man would just ignore the mad Italian woman and mock her.

One day, I was outside when one of his pigeons mistakenly landed in our backyard... They must all look the same from the sky. So I ran in to tell Mum. She came out and said she would sort it out and sent me off to play down the ginnel.

That evening when I came home for dinner, I was surprised to see that we had chicken... We only had chicken on special occasions. Mum explained that the man was so happy to get his bird back that he gave her a reward, which she used to get a lovely chicken. It couldn't have been much money, because the chicken was quite small. Anyway, we were still very grateful and tucked into our feast.

Halfway through my second bite of chicken, I began to think there was something wrong with it. It tasted funny, and it was darker than normal chicken. It still tasted nice though, so I carried on... until, that is, I bit into something metallic. I put my fingers into my mouth and pulled out a thick metal ring. "What the hell is this?"

Mum immediately said: "That's very lucky! Make a wish." She then went on to say that perhaps we shouldn't tell anyone that the pigeon had landed in our backyard, because the owner didn't want anyone to know his pigeons couldn't find their way home. Sounded logical to me...

Haircuts 2

Debbie and I were staying at Mum's for the weekend when Debbie suddenly decided that she needed a hairstyle change... No, don't worry, I didn't let Mum loose on her. No, she decided to go to the local hairdresser's in Manchester. I was waiting at home for her when I heard the door open, then slam shut. I could hear Debbie crying, so I went to see what was wrong, but before I could get there she had disappeared upstairs and locked herself in the bathroom. I spent hours trying to talk her out of there. Apparently, the hairstyle did not turn out the way she had wanted, and she was distraught. I finally got her to open the bathroom door so I could have a look. She had wanted a wavy hairstyle, but what she actually got was very... very tight curls.

I must admit it wasn't her best look, but I managed,

after about thirty minutes of reassurance, to convince her she looked great. She smiled, took my hand and I led her downstairs. As we passed the front door, Mum walked in. She took one look at Debbie's hair... She pulled a disapproving face... Then she said: "Never mind... it will grow out." Debbie burst into tears and spent the rest of the evening in the bathroom.

Graduation day, trains and tunnels

It was the day of my graduation and I went to Manchester to pick Mum up and bring her with me to Liverpool, where I had studied. The graduation was to be held in Liverpool's famous and stunningly beautiful Anglican cathedral. I arranged to take Mum to Liverpool by train. I had done the trip so many times in the previous four years, but it wasn't until we got to the station that I realised this was the first time I could remember taking a train with Mum.

Despite having lived in the UK for so long, she never really went outside her comfort zone. The bus was fine, even taxis, but I don't think she ever used a train. Things that were second nature to me were alien to her and I could see she was nervous about the whole thing. If it hadn't been for the fact that she was going to see her son receive his degree in physics, I don't think she would have stepped on the train. While we were on the platform waiting for the train to arrive I could see that the noise and bustle were overwhelming her, so I said, "Shall we get a coffee to take on the train?"

Mum replied: "If you want." *If you want* was her stock answer to most things, especially if the question was for something that would benefit her.

Armed with coffees and sandwiches, we boarded the train. We found a set of seats facing each other, with a table in between, and settled down. Before the train set off, we were chatting, eating our sandwiches and drinking our coffees. But once we started moving a strange thing began to happen. Every couple of minutes, Mum would hold up her hand and say, "Shhh."

At first I thought I had said something rude, but after the fourth or fifth time, I finally said: "Mum, what's wrong?"

"What do you mean? Nothing's wrong," she said.

I started to second guess myself and thought perhaps I had imagined it; after all, it was a momentous day. So I carried on talking, only to be interrupted with the hand and another shush. Right...! I did not imagine that. "What?" I said. "You keep telling me to be quiet. Why?"

She looked at me with the 'Are you stupid?' look and said: "Because we're going under a bridge."

"What do you mean, because we're going under a bridge?"

Apparently it was bad luck to talk whilst going under a bridge. Of course it is...! How could I be so foolish to have forgotten that!

Do you know how many bridges there are between Manchester and Liverpool? Well, neither do I, but I reckon there must be thirty plus, because for the thirty-minute journey we had to stop talking at least once a minute. Thank God there isn't a superstition for travelling *over* bridges, because whilst looking on the internet I found out that the train from Manchester to Liverpool is famous for travelling over sixty-three bridges... SIXTY-THREE! Oh... and I also found out that you must hold your breath when travelling past a graveyard.

When we got to Liverpool we met up with Debbie and her parents and my brother Mike. A beautiful day was had by all, but after we had finished, I asked Mike if he would take Mum home by car.

Italian Christmas

When I was growing up, Christmas wasn't as big a thing for me as it is now, I think perhaps because the reality never lived up to the hype. When I was really young, we just didn't have the money, so Christmases were not that memorable. As I got older and Mum's financial situation improved, she would have more to spend on presents and food, but it didn't make Christmas more memorable. I think it was because for Mum, it was an opportunity to cook more food. And the better off financially she became, the more food she would serve.

For our first Christmas together, I persuaded Debbie to join me in Manchester. I had no idea what her expectations were; I just thought it would be great for us to be together. Just to give you some context, I went down to join her and her family in Devon the following year and I was just blown away. They celebrated Christmas so well, with all the Dickensian pomp and ceremony I had only seen in films. With all the wonderful food, the traditions... everything... and it was brilliant. If I'd have known that, I would have prepared her for the shock that she was going to get in Manchester.

Christmas Day started the usual way... We were awoken by the complex aromas of a turkey and a full English breakfast. We got dressed and went downstairs, opened our presents and then went straight in for the extra-large full English breakfast. After breakfast we chilled out, went for a walk and looked through our presents again. While we were chilling, Mum was cooking Christmas dinner, which in reality was only going to be in a couple of hours.

Because this was the first Christmas that I had brought home a girlfriend, Mum wanted to make it special, so she invited the whole family for Christmas dinner. Over the next couple of hours, my brothers, sister and their families started arriving. In actual fact it was a very special Christmas, because it was the only time that we had all the families together for dinner.

I think there must have been fifteen of us in total, so we put together some makeshift tables and borrowed some chairs and the festivities began. Mum brought out a never-ending series of dishes, from turkey and ham to roast potatoes, sprouts, cauliflower, peas, mashed potatoes, stuffing... and more. She then came out with a huge turkey bone in one hand, a glass of Marsala wine in the other and a paper party hat on her head. I'm sure this was another of her traditions, but I can't for the life of me remember which and why.

The meal was a success, and everyone was so stuffed we were all slipping into our own personal food comas when in came Mum with Christmas pudding and cream! Everyone groaned, then cheered, but more out of politeness than a need for dessert. As we were finishing the pudding, in she came with Italian coffee and After Eight Mints. I am definitely reminded of Monty Python and the sketch with Mr Creosote, where the waiter offers him a wafer-thin mint and he says: "Fuck off... I couldn't eat another thing," but the waiter encourages him to eat the mint and Mr Creosote explodes... That's exactly how we all felt.

We chatted and laughed over the coffee, wine and beer. Then a fight broke out between two of the kids, which escalated to the mothers fighting. It even came to blows and hair pulling... I must admit I can't remember whether the hair pulling was the mothers or the children. The reason why I can't remember was because in the middle of the fight, Mum came in with ham sandwiches. My brothers and I were happily tucking into the sandwiches when Mum jumped into the melee... Well, all that excitement builds an appetite.

In the middle of all the commotion I turned to Debbie to offer her a sandwich. She was in shock, with eyes wide open and mouth agog... She could not believe what she was witnessing. You've got to understand that arguments and fights are all part of a Hyde family get together, and if you're not involved in the fight, you carry on eating. I hadn't realised that wasn't what happened at most families' meals until Debbie said: "Aren't you going to stop them?"

My brother Chris said, "Don't worry, we'll save them some sandwiches."

Mum eventually separated them and clipped them around the ears, then shoved a plate of sandwiches in their faces. They all grabbed a sandwich and a drink and carried on as though nothing had happened.

Debbie, still in shock, whispered to me: "What is going

on?"

I smiled. "Welcome to the family!"

Who needs a lawn mower when you've got a pair of scissors?

Mum was very proud, stubborn and headstrong, which can be a dangerous combination. I remember a sunny summer's day when we had moved into a new council house that had a garden. We'd never had a garden before and because of that, we had no gardening tools. Mum asked my brother Chris, who was living with his girlfriend at the time, to bring his lawn mower over so she could cut the lawn. Chris said he would do it for her later that afternoon. This seemed to piss Mum off a little, because she wanted to do it now, not later. So, after Chris had left, she started muttering to herself and, armed with a pair of scissors, marched out to the garden and proceeded to cut the grass... blade by blade.

Knowing Chris had offered to mow it that afternoon, I leaned out of the window and asked Mum what she was doing. "Shut up!" Mum said. "I'm not a cripple!"

"Of course, no problem... I'll trim the branches of the tree."

This was at the new council house again. Our neighbour came around one day and pointed out that the tree in our back garden was hanging over his garden. He asked very politely if we could cut the branches back a little, because they were blocking the sun from his favourite seating area. Mum politely said she would sort it out, but as soon as the door closed, she said, "Cheeky bastard!" She then went to the shed in the back garden, which was full of stuff from the previous occupant.

She came out armed with a rusty saw and marched to the offending tree. Looking up, she realised the branches were too high for her to reach. I asked her if she wanted me to do it and she gave her usual reply: "Shut up... I'm not a cripple!"

After ten minutes of unsuccessfully attempting to reach the branches by standing on various chairs and dustbins, she stormed back into the shed. There was more rummaging and swearing, then she emerged red-faced and armed with an axe... an axe! "Mum! What are you doing?" I shouted.

"So the branches are hanging in your garden, are they?" she said, in an angry and sarcastic way. She then proceeded to hack away at the trunk of the tree. Thwack! As far as she was concerned, if she couldn't cut the branches then the bloody tree was coming down. I couldn't believe what I was seeing... Well, I could, because it was my mum. She gave no thought to where she was hacking or where the tree would fall. This was quite evident when it started to tilt towards the neighbour's fence! She tried to push it the other way, but it was too big and heavy. I ran out to help, but as I stepped into the garden, there was an almighty crack and the tree started to fall – straight through the neighbour's fence, only just missing his greenhouse.

Mum turned and walked towards the house. As she passed me, she threw the axe to the floor and said, victoriously: "Well, he doesn't have to worry about the branches blocking the sun anymore."

Resistance is futile

Mum was a compulsive one-woman restaurant. If she couldn't feed you, she felt as though she wasn't performing a task given to her by God. When you turned up at her home, she wouldn't even wait until you had sat down before asking: "Have you eaten?" It was the most redundant question, because whatever you said would be followed by, "I can make some pasta if you want?" If you said you'd only just eaten, she would reply with: "Chips?" If you declined on the grounds that you were full, she would say: "I can make a ham sandwich?" And if you politely refused this, she would say: "Cup of tea?"

To which we would thankfully say: "Yes... that would be great."

Mum would be gone for a while, then return with cups of tea and a huge plate full of ham sandwiches. "I just made them for myself... You can have one if you want."

She was like the Borg from Star Trek... and resistance was futile. And while you were eating the ham sandwiches you didn't want, she would go into the kitchen and start cooking some chips that you didn't want either.

Don't worry... I'll just make her some dry toast

Another incident that has become folklore in our family was when Debbie and I had to leave our eldest daughter, Rebecca, with Mum for a few days. Rebecca couldn't go to her nursery because she was ill and we both had to travel for work. Mum was over the moon to have Rebecca, because she didn't see her that often.

Debbie dropped Rebecca off at Mum's place and said that the doctor had given instructions that she shouldn't have much to eat over the next twenty-four hours. Mum nodded her understanding, but Debbie knew better and said: "Margherita, please don't feed her lots of food. Just some toast and lots of fluids... please."

"Yes, yes, don't worry," Mum said.

We started to worry the next day when Debbie phoned to chat with Mum and Rebecca. She talked initially with Mum and asked her how Rebecca had been. "She's been great... she's fine," Mum said. Debbie asked what she had had to eat and Mum said she'd only had some toast. OK... that sounded good.

So Debbie then asked if she could speak to Rebecca. When she came to the phone, Debbie said: "Hi baby, how are you?" Rebecca said she'd had a relaxing day watching TV. Debbie asked her what she'd had to eat, expecting her to say that all she'd had was some dry toast. "Well... for breakfast I had egg, bacon, sausages, beans and toast, then for lunch I had some pasta with cheese and for dinner I had some chicken and chips." Well... there was nothing we could do about it; we would just have to grin and bear it.

The weekend came and Debbie and I travelled up to Mum's to pick up Rebecca. When we went through the front door and saw Rebecca, we were shocked beyond all belief. When Debbie dropped her off, she was a delicate toddler, but now she looked as though she'd been eating doughnuts every day for the last six months... and she was only with Mum for three days!

Words of Wisdom: Make memories!

Chapter 16

Dementia, Noisy Postmen, Voices in the Walls, Ghosts and Care Homes

Dementia has to be one of the most difficult subjects to tackle when it concerns a parent. Most of us will be unwilling to entertain the possibility, never mind discuss the possible decisions that might have to be made. If there is more than one child it is highly likely that when one of them raises the idea of dementia, one or more of the siblings will refuse to believe there is a problem. Usually the one who notices it is the one who lives closest and has taken on the immediate care duties. The ones that live further away and can't visit as often as they would like tend not to see any issues. This means that the sibling who raised the issue feels like the 'villain'. I have seen this first hand with Mum, and with close friends who have gone through the same process.

After time, things get worse... The parent starts to have more and more accidents. They can often be found wandering the streets in the middle of the night, and they start to ask after family members who have passed away. It's at this point that all siblings finally see the same thing and decide to tackle the difficult next steps together. With the emphasis on the word 'together' – any decisions must be made together, partly to make sure that any doubts are tackled head on, and partly to ensure that no sibling feels individual responsibility for any action... The burden of responsibility must be shared.

As is my way, I would like to describe to you how this happened to our family, but through some funny and not-so-funny stories. During the last twenty years of Mum's life, each of my siblings took their turn to look after her. First it was Mike, when he lived close to her in Manchester. Then, when he and his wife moved to Blackpool, they arranged for Mum to move close to them. Mum was still Mum at this point, although looking back we can see the tell-tale signs of what was to come.

Then Mum moved back to Manchester and Diane looked after her. After Diane moved abroad, Chris took his turn. However, although Diane, Mike and their families helped out during this final period, the majority of the burden fell to Chris and his family. Me? I have always lived away, so never stepped up to the plate when it came to looking after Mum – and I had to come to terms with that guilt... yes, there was, is and always will be guilt. Debbie and I contemplated bringing Mum down to live with us, even though we knew our jobs involved significant travel, which would mean Mum would be on her own a lot. We discussed it with her, and she thought about it for a while, but then she said she didn't want to leave the extended family in Manchester. Although she would love to live with us and see our kids more often, she said she would miss all the other grandkids in Manchester. Deep down, I knew it was a bad idea; it's just that I wanted to help in some way... I wanted to pull my weight.

I have pulled together a set of incidents that span the period from long before we even thought about dementia to the point at which we couldn't ignore it. My hope is that sharing these stories might help people going through similar experiences.

The noisy postman

When Mum moved to Blackpool, she lived on the first floor in a maisonette. It had a nice front garden that she shared with the man who lived in the flat beneath her. On one of our visits to see Mum, we parked the car outside the garden gate, and I let Rebecca and Emma go through first. Well, they tried to go through the gate, but it wouldn't budge. I went up to take a look and realised that it had been wired shut.

I pulled out my phone and called Mum to tell her. "Oh! I forgot... I'm coming down now," she said. She came walking down the garden path and freed the gate to let us in.

"Mum, why did you tie up the gate?" I asked.

"The postman makes so much noise when he delivers the post to the man who lives below me, it wakes me up," she said, "so I tied the gate so he can't come in, and now I can get some rest."

I waited a couple of seconds and said, "You do know that now *you* won't get any post delivered?"

It was a Homer Simpson moment... She thought about it and scrunched up her face, but instead of saying 'D'oh!' she said "Shit!"

The man downstairs is following me

On another visit to her Blackpool flat, things were going as they normally did. Mum made some chips and we sat down to have chip butties. She asked if we wanted a drink and then walked towards the kitchen, but on the way she stamped on the floor and muttered something under her breath. When she came back with the drinks, I had to ask her why she stamped on the floor.

"That man downstairs is driving me mad! He keeps following me everywhere I go," she said.

Debbie and I looked at each other, then back at Mum. With a smile on my face, I said, "What do you mean? He's not going to be following you."

She got angry. "Yes...! Every night when I get up to go to the toilet, I can hear him following me downstairs... but last night I fooled him." She smiled. "I went to the toilet as usual, but when I finished I walked into the front room, then tip-toed back to the bedroom... That showed him." She started to giggle to herself, as did we, but... If we had been more informed about dementia, perhaps this would have rung alarm bells.

The man next door is following me

When Mum came back to Manchester she moved into a warden-controlled bungalow. She still looked after herself, but she had a big red emergency button that would alert a nearby warden if she needed help. This was a great comfort to us, knowing that she could summon help any time of the day or night.

Things really started to deteriorate here, and it ceased to be funny any more. On one of our regular visits, we could tell Mum was distressed. She kept going on about the man next door and how he followed her night and day. She said she had to cover all the power sockets on the wall that faced his property, because he was watching her through the sockets. She said he was making noises all night and keeping her awake. The warden had put in a noise recording system for twenty-four hours, but it had revealed no loud noises or anything out of the ordinary. Mum had even called the police in, but while the officer was taking notes, he got a call on the radio. Mum said she couldn't trust him because he was talking to the man next door.

Don't sit there, the dogs are sat there

Then came the ghosts... Mum was convinced there were two mischievous dogs who now lived with her in the front room. Mid-conversation, she would point to them and tell us they were up to something. Or say, "Don't sit there, the dogs are sat there." It was so sad to see... She would also keep asking the same question over and over again. Then she said she hadn't phoned her brother in Italy for a while, and I had to tell her that he had died the year before.

The last bowl of chips

However, those incidents, no matter how disturbing, were nothing compared to this one, and even now it breaks my heart to recount it. Debbie and I were working in Manchester for a couple of days and decided to pop in and see Mum. She looked frail, but she still asked if we wanted some chips and we gratefully said yes. So she went into the kitchen to start off a batch of chips. She came back into the front room and we chatted, with her getting up every now and then to check on the chips. After about the sixth or seventh trip to the kitchen she said they were taking ages but should be ready soon. Debbie was getting worried and she asked me to check on the chips. When I got to the kitchen, I saw a pan full of chips in a bath of rancid black oil, which was just frothing away...

That was the last time she ever cooked chips for us... It makes me want to cry.

After the chips incident, I had a long chat with Chris, after which he booked an appointment with the doctor to have Mum assessed for dementia. It wasn't just about her mental ability; her body was deteriorating fast too. She was always in pain and could barely walk now.

Later that week she was assessed, and the doctor confirmed advanced dementia. He recommended a course of drugs that would, he said, suppress the hallucinations and reduce her stress levels. He also recommended that she should be placed in a care home. Chris was concerned about all of us agreeing to this, but there was no other solution for either Mum or him. His health had started to deteriorate too, and there was no way he could continue to care for Mum the way he had. Mike and I agreed straight away. We knew it was the only way that Mum could get the care she now needed. Diane was the one who went through the most anguish, because Mum had asked her to promise many years ago that she wouldn't put her in a care home. And now here she was, needing to make an unenviable decision about the very thing she had promised she would never do. However, she knew Mum's quality of life was deteriorating quickly, and, with heavy heart, she agreed.

The next time we visited Mum was in the care home. Chris had prepared us for the fact that she was now heavily sedated and had very few occasions where she was lucid, but nothing could have prepared us for the sight that awaited us. We buzzed the intercom and said who we were, and a nurse came to the door to let us in. She asked us to sign into the visitors' book and then make our way into the conservatory area, where we would find Mum. While we were signing in, an old woman came up to the door and smiled at us. She had her coat on and a handbag over her arm. "I'm waiting to be picked up by my daughter... She's taking me home to live with her," she said. We all smiled and said that was lovely, but we later learned that there was no daughter and she did this every day.

We went through to the main seating area, where everyone was watching TV, and through to the conservatory, where we found Mum in a wheelchair, facing a window that looked out onto the garden. She was like a china doll, all curled up and so frail. She looked up and recognised me... then burst into tears. She tried to speak, but just couldn't remember how to say what she wanted to say. She was in pain and just couldn't get comfortable... I was terrified to touch her, because I thought she might break.

I remember looking around at the other residents: most were like Mum, just gazing into the distance, but some were watching us and smiling, and a couple were shouting obscenities at anyone who came into view. I thought to myself, "What have we done?" I knew there was nothing else we could have done at the time... but that didn't help. What a dilemma... to have the hallucinations that haunt you and stress you, twenty-four hours a day, or to live in a foggy state where you don't quite know what's going on. Neither were acceptable as far as I could see, yet no one could offer an alternative.

I have been pondering this point for some time now and I believe there is an alternative, but it requires a fundamental change to what is deemed normal and important in our society. In the past, you grew up in the town where your parents were born. You got a job close by, you married and lived in the same town, and so did your children. Grandparents were always a part of this big family unit; they had a role to play and they felt as though they were valued. It gave them a purpose and kept their minds active. As jobs became harder to find locally, the family unit became fragmented as sons and daughters left their home town to seek a life elsewhere. This has resulted in more and more grandparents becoming isolated and feeling that they no longer have a role to play.

Any website on dementia will say that keeping your mind active reduces your risk of getting dementia. The number of times I used to visit Mum and she would be staring into space... I can't help thinking that if she had more to occupy her time, she might not have deteriorated as badly as she did.

The two countries that have the oldest populations are

Japan and Italy. In both these countries, the elderly are held in great regard. In Italy, family is seen as the core to life. Grandparents don't just play a key role in the family unit, they also play a key role in family businesses and have their own social scene. They are valued and kept active. Whenever I had Mum over to stay with us, I would do everything for her. I would not let her cook or clean up, despite her always asking. I thought I was being kind to her by letting her relax and be pampered, but in actual fact I was taking away her role and her purpose.

Once I realised this, on the last few times she visited I would let her do the ironing, cleaning and anything else she wanted... and I could see the change immediately – she smiled more and gave us glimpses of her old self. It may have been too little, too late for my mum, but perhaps the more people that read this book, the more chance there is that other mums and dads could benefit...?

As I write this paragraph, we are just coming out of our third COVID-19 lockdown in the UK. If we put aside the immeasurable heartache of those who have lost loved ones to the virus, it has given us a glimpse of a better way of life... a return to an older, simpler way of life. During lockdown, more of us have been working from home. There have been fewer cars on the road, fewer people taking flights. The environmentalists will point to an improvement in air and water quality. The canals of Venice became clear for the first time in recent history, and wildlife has ventured into the cities. On a more local scale, we find ourselves thinking about and buying more local produce. People who either lost their jobs or wanted to do something more meaningful have created 'pop-up' bakeries, delicatessens, farm shops etc... and have been delivering to our doorstep.

This has given me a greater appreciation for community, which will stay with me long after lockdown has finished. I now consciously look to support my local community and buy local wherever possible. It feels good to see the face of the person I am buying from; it feels good to see their appreciation. Don't get me wrong, I also like and benefit from the global corporations that deliver products to my door, but that doesn't mean we can't have both.

Lockdown would have been very different if it wasn't for the advances in our communication technology. Those of us who have been fortunate enough to be allowed to work from home during the pandemic have experienced what it would be like to work locally. We have had the pleasure of not spending hours of our precious time commuting each week. We have had the pleasure of meeting our loved ones next to the coffee machine for a chat each day... although I must admit that some of my friends don't see that as pleasure. Many companies have made a commitment to keep this way of working after lockdown. They have seen the benefits – both socially and commercially – of having a partly remote workforce.

I'd like to think there will be a permanent change to society as we emerge from the pandemic. I'd like to think that more of us will live and work locally. I'd like to think that the family unit will stay closer together. I'd like to think that more grandparents will feel useful and needed for longer. I'd like to think that more grandparents will stay active for longer. And I'd like to think that maybe, just maybe, fewer of them will have to suffer the effects of dementia. It's a nice thought...

Words of Wisdom: Everyone needs to feel useful and wanted.

Chapter 17

The Legacy

My mother lived a hard life... and, to the outsider, it would appear to be a life full of pain and struggles. I would forgive anyone who thought "What was the point? So much suffering... for what?!" Yes, there was suffering, but there was so much love, laughter and smiles. There was food... there was reheated pasta... there was pizza... there was gnocchi that could sink a battleship. There was ice cream... there were greasy witches... there was racing pigeon pie... there was the perfect cup of coffee. She left behind a legacy that will live forever.

She raised four children, who gave her many grandchildren, who in turn gave and continue to give her many great-grandchildren, who in turn will... well, you get my drift. Being responsible for a large and ever-growing family tree would be enough to give anyone a sense of achievement and self-worth. But she left so much more than just a family tree... She left behind a legacy of memories and principles that her children will not only pass down to their children, but will also go on to influence everyone they meet.

She didn't preach a way of life, she just lived her life the only way she knew how. She was a product of her upbringing, her trials and tribulations... and, of course, the

Italian mamma's genetic memory. She wasn't a saint or the easiest person to live with, but she was consistent. She lived by her firm principles and sometimes that is more important than what those principles actually were. Having principles that you stick to lets other people know they can rely on you. They know what you are likely to do and how you are going to react. They know that, no matter what happens, you will hold to your principles. This gives people confidence... it gives them a *lighthouse* in a rough sea... you will always be right where they need you to be.

What were my mother's principles? Well, when I started to analyse them they were all eclipsed by one motto: 'Family is everything. Sacrifice everything for your family.' Mum sacrificed so much for her family and the people she loved. I always remember her giving up anything she had if it would make others happy. This didn't mean she was a soft touch... far from it. If you thought you had sweet-talked her into giving you all the money in her purse, then you would have been sorely mistaken. If she gave you something, it would be because she wanted to. The fact that you were using deception to get what you wanted meant you needed it... and if she loved you and you needed something, then she would give it to you, even if it was everything she had. I was going to say she sacrificed her own happiness to make others happy, but I don't think that's entirely true. She gained happiness from making others happy, and I can say with the utmost confidence that she never expected anything in return.

She was the *lighthouse* in our family. If ever you were in trouble, you knew she would always be there for you. You knew that if you came home saying an army of blood-thirsty demons were outside and wanted to eat you alive, she would roll up her sleeves and go out to face them. And if you asked me who I'd put my money on... it would be my mum. It's that last point that had the most impact on my life. If my daughters watched me get into a boxing ring with someone half my age, they would confidently expect me to get punched to a pulp. But if they were surrounded by an army of blood-thirsty demons, they would say: "You'd better be afraid, because my dad is coming."

It has always been my desire to be the *lighthouse* of my family, as it is and was for my brothers and sister. We will pass this on to all our children, and their children will do the same. What a wonderful place the world would be if there were *lighthouses* as far as the eye could see... Now that's a legacy.

I'll leave you with two of my favourite Italian sayings.

The first represents how I feel about family: "Chi si volta, e chi si gira, sempre a casa va finire," which translates as "**No matter where you go or turn, you'll always end up home.**"

The second is a wonderful phrase we found in one of Mum's letters from her brother Attilio. He finished the letter with: "Mi fermo con la penna, ma non con il cuore," which translates as "**I stop with the pen, but not with the heart.**"

Words of Wisdom: Be the best lighthouse you can be.

Words of Wisdom

Look beneath the surface, because under the most intimidating exterior can often be found the warmest and most amazing souls.

One of my favourite lyrics are from a Bob Marley song: "You never know how strong you are, until being strong is the only choice you have."

All it takes to earn the eternal love of a dog is a biscuit and a hug... but to earn the love of a child you need a lifetime of sacrifice.

There is wonderment in the seemingly mundane... so just remember that the next time you look at your mum or dad. You don't really know them or what they have been through or even what they do now.

Life is, as the song says "a rollercoaster..." It's full of ups and downs, twists and turns... love and happiness... joy and sadness... and tears for all occasions. It's easy to get lost in the ride while staring at the tracks ahead. Take time to turn around and look at the people who are in the car with you... and appreciate what you have.

Always make sure you have a supply of salt, rice, iron and brooms.

When someone says they have a great idea, run away! But make sure you don't miss the Star Trek moments in life.

It's easy to think that everything in your life is bad or going wrong... but just remember that every now and then you get to go to the toilet without being attacked by rats.

When presented with a no-win situation, pretend to be dead.

Never give up on your search for the perfect cup of coffee.

Make time to share good food and good wine with family and friends... and you will have memories that will keep you warm on the coldest of nights.

If you put a sign up next to a red button that says: "Do not push this red button," then you can be pretty sure that someone is going to push the red button.

Enjoy the free ice cream while it lasts, because it won't always be there.

Garlic is the devil's bum juice and the domain of the unimaginative cook.

You don't need money to have love and self-respect. You can do incredible things if you put your mind to it – and money can make you happy.

Make memories!

Everyone needs to feel useful and wanted.

Be the best lighthouse you can be.

Acknowledgements

I'd like to thank my mum for always being there for me.

I'd like to thank my brother Chris for letting me shine.

Thanks to Mike, Diane, Debbie, Rebecca and Rosemary for their help in piecing together Mum's story.

I'd like to thank Zeppie, Chris and Juju for letting me tell Auntie Pina's story.

And I'd like to thank Emma, Sam Nero and Paola Giglio for their help with my research on Italian culture and migration.

Finally, thanks to *Atlas Obscura* for writing the article 'Sex, Drugs, and Broomsticks: The Origins of the Iconic Witch', because it shows that my mother wasn't totally mad.

More From The Author

The Leukaemia Diaries:
Seeing the funnier side of cancer

The Leukaemia Diaries: Seeing the Funnier Side of Cancer, details Anthony's journey from just before being diagnosed with Chronic Myeloid Leukaemia (CML) to the scary 'I'm going to die' bit, to the joys of chemotherapy, getting back to work and beyond. It is an emotional, honest and heartfelt account that not only aims to engage, entertain and inform, but also comfort and inspire. It gives family and friends an idea of what their loved ones are going through and what's going through their mind at such a traumatic and terrifying time.

Available in paperback and for Kindle.

Coming Soon

The Italian Cookbook:
It's a Family Thing

Keep an eye on Anthony's website for more details:

www.adhyde.com

About the Author

Anthony Hyde is a second-generation Italian who grew up on the cobbled streets of Manchester... well, when he says on, he really means close by... in a house. He spent most of his childhood watching sci-fi/fantasy movies and fishing for newts and sticklebacks in the local canal. He dreamt of going to university, meeting and marrying the girl of his dreams, settling down to have a family and living happily ever after... and, of course, becoming an astronaut with magical powers.

One by one his dreams started to come true: he graduated with a degree in physics, met and married the girl of his dreams and had two beautiful girls. Unfortunately, while he was living happily ever after, he was diagnosed with Chronic Myeloid Leukaemia.

This event awakened the writer's voice within him and gave him the inspiration to write The Leukaemia Diaries, which is a light-hearted and inspirational account of his experiences from just before being diagnosed with CML through treatment and beyond.

In addition to building his back catalogue with books like The Mamma Nero Diaries and The Italian Cookbook, he is also working hard on his remaining dreams... especially the one where he develops magical powers.

Website: www.adhyde.com
Facebook: www.facebook.com/ADHydeAuthor
Twitter: twitter.com/adhydeauthor
Instagram: www.instagram.com/adhydeauthor/